Your Own Business: From Concept to Success

HELEN BEARE was born in 1963 in Plymouth. After a degree in French and German at Cambridge University, she worked for a firm of chartered accountants in London, later specializing in working with smaller businesses and in business planning. She now lives near Buckingham, working with her partner in a chartered accountancy practice established by him in 1989. She has written one other book for Sheldon Press, *How to Avoid Business Failure* (1993).

Sheldon Business Books

Sheldon Business Books is a list which exists to promote and facilitate the adoption of humane values and equal opportunities integrated with the technical and commercial expertise essential for successful business practice. Both practical and theoretical issues which challenge today's workforce will be explored in jargon-free, soundly researched books.

The first titles in the series are:
Making Change Work for You by Alison Hardingham
Taking the Macho Out of Management by Paddy O'Brien
How to Succeed in Psychometric Tests by David Cohen
Fit to Work by Paddy O'Brien
How to Avoid Business Failure by Helen Beare
Beyond Total Quality Management by Larry Reynolds
Making Successful Presentations by Patrick Forsyth

Helen Beare # Your Own Business

From Concept to Success

Sheldon Business Books

First published in Great Britain 1995
Sheldon Press, SPCK, Marylebone Road, London NW1 4DU

British Library Cataloguing-in-Publication Data
A catalogue record for this book is available from
the British Library
ISBN 0-85969-714-2

Photoset by Deltatype Ltd, Ellesmere Port, Cheshire
Printed in Great Britain by the Cromwell Press, Melksham, Wilts

Contents

1 **Before you do anything . . .**

Setting up in business would be infinitely easier – and far less challenging – if there were a blueprint which guaranteed success. In reality, life is never that simple. But you can take steps to give your business the best possible chance of success by making sure that you plan it properly and control it effectively.

This book looks at many of the issues, business and personal, which you will have to confront both before and after you get your venture off the ground, drawing on the successes and difficulties experienced by a variety of small businesses and the lessons which they have learned. It will not solve your business problems for you, but together with your own enthusiasm and commitment it will help you to develop an effective approach to running your own business.

Making the decision to set up your own business is an enormous step to take, and the implications – not to mention the changes to your life – should never be underestimated, however confident you feel about your chances of success. Many small and new businesses do not succeed. Although an element of fortune may well play a part, you can avoid many pitfalls by ensuring that you have thought through properly both your business idea and what being in business will entail, *before* you take the plunge. A large number of small businesses which fail in the early stages should never have been set up in the first place: their owners were either ill-equipped to run a business or had not given any serious consideration to the practical or financial implications.

Many are also successful:

A dressmaker started her business on a part-time, small-scale basis, designing and making evening and wedding dresses and 'special occasion' clothes. She began by working for friends and acquaintances, to test both the demand for and the response to her skills. Gradually, the personal recommendations began to spread, the volume of work increased and she began to advertise more widely. Her business expanded slowly but steadily, she took on part-time help and subsequently opened a small shop. Her business is now thriving; she recommends an approach that combines enthusiasm, dedication and, above all, an awareness of the reality of being in business.

In complete contrast, a car valeting service was set up by a former car mechanic, who believed that the 'home' service he offered would be a strong enough selling feature to make the business a success. Although his customers were delighted with his work, he had not carried out any research beforehand into the likely demand for his service. He discovered that he was unable to generate sufficient work, although he advertised over a wide local area. He gave up his business after only a year, and now regrets having not devoted more time to thinking about how it could be made to work before committing his time and resources to the venture.

Nobody can foresee every single problem which will arise. However, you can achieve a vast amount by thinking about and trying to resolve issues in advance, whether they are financial, technical, logistical or personal.

Why do you want to set up in business?

You might have very clear and positive reasons for starting your own business. Alternatively, you might be toying with the idea for more negative reasons, such as disliking your current job or career path. Starting your own business should never be seen purely as an escape: being your own boss will, in some ways, be far more difficult – although in other ways it can be very much more satisfying.

Try to analyse your reasons for wanting to run your own business. This will help to focus your mind on both the positive and negative aspects of your thinking, and highlight the more problematic issues which need to be resolved before you take any action to get the business off the ground. For example:

- Do you have an idea for a new concept or product?
- Do you want to be your own boss?
- Are you trying to make a better living?
- Does redundancy leave you with little alternative to self-employment?
- Are you dissatisfied because you feel you are under-achieving/under-paid/undervalued/overworked in your current job?
- Do you want to be *seen* as a successful entrepreneur?

All of the above reasons have positive and negative implications in varying proportions. Ask your spouse, partner or a business associate to discuss your thoughts with you and to point out the problems and disadvantages as you put forward your case for wanting to start your own business. Having your ideas critically examined can be very helpful.

The following pages do not intend to discourage you, but rather aim to play the role of devil's advocate, to help you to be as honest with yourself as possible about your reasons for starting your own business. All of the reasons and scenarios described below are based on fact not fiction. It is surprisingly common for people to admit eventually that at least part of their motivation for setting up in business was based on highly subjective factors.

New concept or product

From the experience and expertise you have gained in your current job or field, perhaps you have become aware of a gap in the market which you believe you can fill. This might be for a completely new product or service, or an extension or adaptation of an existing one. The development of a brand new product can be the most risky path to take, since it is likely to require both more capital and more time to become established in its market than you will anticipate at the outset. Alternatively, if you have identified a means of improving an existing product or service, you will have a significant edge over your competitors.

A director of a transport business specializing in the entertainment industry, which arranged the movement of fragile equipment all over the world, found himself in this situation. Through contact and discussions with a business associate, he believed he had found a means of upgrading the quality of flight cases so that they were stronger and lighter than any existing product on the market.

Although experienced in his field, he had little experience in the day-to-day running of a business himself. The project would also require capital for materials and equipment in the early stages, with no guarantee of any return. Additionally, the time needed for market research and seeking out sales leads was far more than the director could spare whilst still in his current employment.

He eventually decided, after consultation with his family, that to abandon his existing career for this project was too great a risk at this stage. Instead, he and his associate decided to spend a further year researching the market, securing finance and organizing the manufacture of prototypes in whatever time was available to them. After a year, they felt it was safer to proceed with the project on a full-time basis.

Not all decisions will be this difficult, although if you are in employment and will need to give up your job to concentrate on running your business, a great deal of research will be required to assess the risks involved. If you are intending to sell a service rather than a new product, continuing in employment during the initial stages of setting up the business may be easier, but do not underestimate the time that will be required to carry out your research properly. Some guidelines on the issues you will need to consider before setting up your business are set out in chapter 2.

Remember that the vast majority of new businesses do not depend on a completely original product or service. It will of course be helpful if yours has one or more distinguishing features (new or otherwise) which can be used as a selling point and might help to give you an edge over your competitors.

Be your own boss

Many people are attracted by the idea of being their own boss, and this is often a strong motivating factor in a desire to set up in business. Thoughts of being able to take your own decisions without pressures from colleagues, structuring your day and the hours you work yourself, being free of the 'politics' of being an employee and running the business as you think best can all be extremely appealing. You may have felt that if only you were in charge, the business which employs you would be managed far more effectively.

All of these points have positive aspects. However, also be aware that you will need to be absolutely committed to your business: you will need the self-discipline and enthusiasm to motivate yourself, because nobody else will do it for you. Working hours may be long, your income may drop substantially, taking time off for holidays may become difficult, and you may feel isolated without the company and support of colleagues. If you have previously worked for fairly large businesses, you may have taken for granted the individuals or departments providing specialist skills – finance, advertising and marketing, sales, technical support and so on. If you intend to be in business on your own, you will now need to fill these roles yourself, with guidance and advice from external experts whose services you will have to pay for.

Make a better living

You may feel that by running your own business you will make a better living than you can achieve in paid employment. If this is your only or overriding motivation for wanting to set up your own business, do not set your hopes too high for the short term. The desire to achieve financial security – or just to avoid financial insecurity – can be a powerful motivator, but do not underestimate the financial risks you will be taking.

In the early stages you may eat into any savings you have managed to accumulate in order to get the business off the ground, for the purchase of equipment or goods for resale to customers for example. It may be some time before you are in a position to receive any money from customers or clients.

You may need to cut back your personal and domestic expenditure in the short term, particularly if yours is the main or only source of income in the household. It is essential that this is thought through in detail before setting up your business: there is no point in expending large sums of money on state-of-the-art equipment or a smart car for your business if you are subsequently unable to meet your mortgage repayments. Keeping your financial ambitions realistic will also help to avoid the disillusionment which can sap your motivation.

Redundancy

You may be tempted to set up your own business following redundancy, especially if your chances of securing new employment in the short or medium term seem poor. Your redundancy settlement might suffice to cover the initial expenditure required to get the business started, but do ensure that enough money is set aside to cover your normal domestic and personal expenditure as well, especially if yours is the main or only source of income.

Do think very carefully before deciding to go ahead and set up the business, particularly if considerable expenditure will be required. If this is not the case – perhaps you are selling your time or you already own the necessary tools or equipment – the financial risks will be much reduced.

Even if you regard starting your own business as the only alternative to being out of work, do still take time to think through the effects of your action and take professional advice to ensure that your financial and tax affairs are properly managed.

A hairdresser made redundant from a high street salon started business as a mobile hairdresser. Her initial outgoings for equipment were relatively low; she already owned a car and she was able both to secure the loyalty of some of her existing clients and to build up a base of new local clients from low-cost advertising in newsagents' windows. Although earning slightly less than she had previously, she managed to make a reasonable living. However, although she was generating sufficient income to live on, she had ignored advice received from a friend to put aside gradually enough money to meet her income tax and National Insurance payments when they fell due. She knew well in advance what these would amount to, but having used up the last of her redundancy settlement, she simply hoped that she would be able to find the money she needed at the appropriate time. Although the sum was not that large, she was eventually forced to negotiate an overdraft to pay the liability on time, which led to a further drain on her finances in the form of bank charges and interest.

In retrospect, she knows that she could easily have avoided these problems by listening to the advice she received; she realized this at the time, but kept putting off action until another day.

Dissatisfaction with current job

General dissatisfaction with your current job is not a good reason to set up in business on your own. Beware 'the grass is greener . . .' theory. Anyone who believes that their work problems will suddenly be solved if they set up their own business is likely to be disappointed. Do you feel overworked and underpaid? That your employer does not value you at all and that you could achieve more for yourself elsewhere? If you have a skill or trade which you can use on a self-employed basis, you might be tempted to see this as the obvious escape from your job. However, you need more positive reasons for being in business on your own if you are to succeed – or to be happy – in managing your own business. There is a huge difference between a positive ambition to be your own boss and seeing it as the lesser of two evils.

If these are your primary reasons for setting up your own business, think again. You will be well advised not to take any rash decisions or actions (like resigning from your job) until you have spent considerably more time thinking about whether you *really* want to be in business on your own. Remember the responsibilities and the insecurity of the early stages. If you do not take the time to resolve properly the reasons why you want to set up your business and think through the operational practicalities, you may well find that not only do you struggle to make the business work, but that it also causes you far greater heartache and distress than a job which you dislike.

Image of successful entrepreneur

There are some people whose main motivation for starting their own business is a desire to create an image of a self-sufficient and successful entrepreneur, who is regarded with admiration for their apparent achievements by friends and business associates.

Of course, every person running their own small business wants to see it as a successful one, in terms of providing a stable income, of building up a strong customer or client base and so on. However, if your reasons for starting your business are based largely around a vague ambition to be perceived as the owner of an instantly successful and fast-growing business then you are likely to suffer disillusion and disappointment. The idea of driving a smart car, working in a luxurious office and generally presenting an image of yourself and your business as an overnight success story may be an attractive one, but do not ever be tempted to delude yourself into thinking that you can achieve this either quickly or without a great deal of hard work. If you do choose in the early stages of your business to spend money you cannot really afford on building up an image rather than creating a stable business, you are also likely to increase your chances of business failure. Be realistic: many business failures occur because their owners were not prepared to open their eyes to the realities of business management until it was too late.

Do you know what you are trying to achieve?

It is likely that the goals you set for yourself and your business will overlap with your original reasons for wanting to start the business. However, you may well lose sight of those reasons, especially in the early months of trading on your own, so having shorter- and longer-term goals for your business will give you positive aims to work towards. This will be especially important when you are feeling exposed and tired, and are wondering whether you made the right decision. Your goals may be quite ambitious or relatively modest, but this is less important than the fact that you have tangible aims to work towards after your initial enthusiasm is wearing off. Your goals will also be a vital factor in decisions about the future development of your business, and will be incorporated in your business plan, which is discussed in chapter 3.

Make a list of your aims, then rank them in order of importance. If you are starting in business entirely on your own and need the support of your family, ensure that they are involved in the process. They will find it much easier to give you their full support if they are asked for their opinions and, more importantly, have them taken into serious consideration. On the other hand, if they are happier for you to determine your goals without their input, it is still important for you to make clear to them what those goals are.

Your goals might include:

- to make a reasonable living;
- to improve significantly your standard of living;
- to improve the quality of your life – hours worked, avoid commuting etc.;
- to become the market leader in your field;
- to achieve a target turnover or net profit within a given time-scale;
- to develop a product or service to a particular standard which you have not been able to achieve in your previous employment;

- to develop and create a completely new product or service;
- to retire or sell the business by the age of, say, 50.

Although it is important for you to be the main motivating force behind your aims and plans for your business, it is a good idea to discuss them with friends or trusted business associates, whether or not they have experience in running their own business. They will be able to take a more objective viewpoint and may have ideas which you had not considered – perhaps a potential target market which you had overlooked or were unaware of, or a means of making your product or service significantly more attractive to customers.

You may be the type of person who has a very clear vision for your business, and who does not find it difficult to map out plans and goals for the short and medium term. However, for most people, the process of discussion and gradual revision and refinement of their plans is an extremely valuable one; it can help you to feel both more confident and more enthusiastic about what you are trying to achieve.

It is also essential to reassess your goals from time to time. Do not feel forced to adhere rigidly to your original plans if these no longer seem appropriate. For example, if you find that achieving your target level of turnover will mean working unacceptably long hours, and your financial needs do not demand this level of turnover, do not be afraid to revise your targets.

Have you thought of the implications?

Being in business on your own might bring immediate benefits, such as independence and freedom to make your own decisions, but there may also be times when you feel overwhelmed by the responsibilities that you have taken on. Being aware of these responsibilities and deciding how to cope with them will help you face them with more equanimity when your confidence and enthusiasm are at a low ebb.

Lack of security

No longer will you receive fixed weekly or monthly pay. If you don't work for a month, your business will generate no income that month. If yours is the sole source of income in a household, it will help if you are able to build up a buffer of savings before you set up your business, which will help to tide you over the first few months. Mortgage repayments, domestic bills and so on still have to be paid, even if the business is struggling.

It is essential that your spouse, partner, family and any others who will be directly affected by the change in your income understand the financial implications and are prepared to be supportive. It is a good idea to prepare a household budget. Break it down into periodic payments – annual, quarterly, monthly, weekly and so on. Include a provision for contingencies and emergencies. It might help for some payments, such as insurance premiums, which are often made annually, to be paid monthly instead in order to spread the cashflow.

Quite apart from financial security, you may also feel, especially in the early months, that you are very exposed. Support which may previously have been taken for granted from colleagues or your boss will no longer be there. There may be some issues for which you need specialist guidance, but the running of the business will be dependent on you entirely. Your spouse or partner and family will need to be aware of the level of stress which this can lead to.

> An engineer who had been in business on his own for several years found that he was beginning to suffer from the effects of a lack of the security which he had previously been able to take for granted. The nature of his work was in itself stressful; it called for a high level of technical precision and he had never been able to 'switch off' at the end of the working day. Although the business was not suffering any financial difficulty, his temperament meant that he worried constantly about winning new contracts, whether his clients would pay him, and what would happen if he were unable to afford his loan repayments. Inevitably, his domestic life as well as both his physical and mental well-being began to suffer. He managed to resolve his problems gradually, first by admitting his tendency to worry. He also learnt to discuss his fears more openly with his family, so that they were no longer bottled up or able to grow out of all proportion to their actual significance.

Legal and financial responsibilities

Depending on the type of business you are running, there may be specific regulations which must be followed strictly, such as those which apply to any food preparation or catering business. You will be responsible for ensuring that you have researched properly and applied these regulations, taking specialist advice if there are issues which you are unsure about.

Never be tempted to think that you can avoid or side-step such regulations, because it seems too inconvenient or time-consuming to deal with them properly. You would regret it bitterly if your business were shut down as a result. Don't cut corners!

You will also have the responsibility for ensuring that your accounts and tax affairs are dealt with properly. Don't put off finding an accountant in whom you have confidence – he or she may well be able to help you with issues which you had overlooked, or take some of the burden of dealing with your accounting books or records. Coping with accounting and administration is dealt with in more detail in chapter 4.

If you decide to trade as a limited company, there are also specific issues which apply to company directors, and this is covered in chapter 2.

Do you have the resources?

Finance is not the only resource needed to set up in business; you need to consider your own skills and expertise. Finance is, of course, vital (see chapter 3), but people often underestimate the range of different skills which are involved in running a small business. You will not be an expert in all of them, but you need to be aware beforehand of those areas in which you are both strongest and weakest and when you will require outside help.

Some of the most important areas in which you need to ask yourself whether you have, or have access to, adequate resources include:

- experience in your chosen business field;
- business experience;
- a sufficiently broad range of skills and expertise;
- finance;
- personal qualities and support.

Do you have experience in your chosen business field?

You may have chosen to set up your business in a field which is already familiar to you, using a skill which you have developed over a number of years. However comprehensive your experience, you may still need to work hard at keeping up to date with new developments in your field. Specialist training courses may be available, or you may need to rely on trade journals. You will need to be especially careful if your field is periodically subject to changes in legislation: it is easy to become out of touch with changes without realizing it, simply because you no longer have the automatic support network which your employer previously provided.

If you have chosen to set up your business in a field in which you have no previous experience, there will be an even greater need to carry out thorough and detailed research before making any move to get the business started. You may believe that in spite of your lack of experience, you have identified a need in a particular market which you can fulfil. However, you are likely to have more difficulty convincing others – such as potential providers of finance or customers – that you have the necessary experience to make a success of your venture. You will have to rely on your more general business skills and your personal characteristics to convince these people that you are the right person to be running this business.

A computer software trainer specializing in word-processing packages, with some limited experience of other applications, became aware of his lack of experience the hard way. Working within a training organization, he became disillusioned with his hours of work, the limited prospects of furthering his career and lack of financial reward, although his job did offer stability and financial security for the foreseeable future.

He felt his work would be more rewarding, both financially and professionally, if he set up his own business. Still relatively inexperienced, he had not yet had a chance to build up a network of professional or client contacts, but believed he had sufficient experience to get by, and would compensate with his excellent interpersonal skills. He felt that running his own business could not be all that difficult, and did not devote too much concern to the implications of self-employment.

He soon discovered that although the clients he secured were happy with his abilities as a trainer, the breadth of training courses and tuition he was able to offer were too limited. The large companies to whose employees he had previously provided training had remained loyal to the training organization he had left. The new clients he acquired, smaller businesses and self-employed individuals, demanded a much broader and more varied range of software training, which he did not have the experience to provide, despite his expertise in his own field.

He was forced into a position where he needed to gain very quickly a detailed knowledge of a much broader range of software if he was to survive, which would require both time and money.

He admits now that he had not properly thought through this deficiency in his skills, simply because it had never previously arisen. Although it was a problem he was able to remedy fairly quickly, he feels he would not have been able to survive in self-employment if his partner had not provided the household with a regular and adequate income. He regards himself as extremely fortunate not to have been forced out of business.

Do you have business experience?

Perhaps you have already worked for a fairly small business, and have some experience in a management capacity within a small business environment. You may feel that you have a reasonably good idea of what to expect when you set up on your own. You may have friends who run their own business, and can talk to them and benefit from their experiences and mistakes. However well informed you feel you are, working for yourself will come as a shock.

You will have to deal with a number of tasks in which you probably have little previous experience, such as finding and negotiating with suppliers, organizing your advertising, finding customers or clients and securing their custom, dealing with your bank manager and so on.

There is no magic formula to success in business management. You may wish to find out about courses aimed specifically at those who are starting up in business on their own. Your local Training and Enterprise Council (TEC) might be a good starting-point: most TECs run general courses as well as seminars on specific areas of business management, and should be able to offer both training and counselling if you need it.

Do not be too proud to ask advice from friends or associates who have set up their own business, or from specialists when necessary. If you can enlist the willing assistance of, say, your partner, perhaps with bookkeeping, invoicing or correspondence, then this might help to spread the work and create more time for you to spend on other aspects of the business.

Do you have the necessary range of skills and expertise?

One of the greatest shocks to many new business owner-managers is the discovery of the broad range of skills and abilities that you are suddenly expected to demonstrate, regardless of your previous experience. These will include:

- a reasonable level of business 'sense';
- the self-discipline to work effectively on your own initiative;
- the ability to deal with people on a number of different levels;
- the imagination to create a new product or service, where relevant;
- specialist professional or technical skills, support and/or training.

Obviously, the list is not exhaustive and additional skills you will require may depend on the type of business you intend to operate.

Try to make your own list, and assess realistically whether you have the necessary skills. If not, do you have access to them elsewhere? Alternatively, are there training courses that can provide you with at least a basic grounding in the areas in which you are weakest? Even the best qualified and experienced expert in a given field can fail in business if insufficient attention is paid to the additional skills required to manage a business effectively.

Do you have the finance?

The finance required to start up your business might be considerable if you need to buy equipment or premises; or it might be relatively small if you are selling a skill and are able to work from home. However much finance you need, you must assess your requirements in detail. If you are unable to provide sufficient finance yourself you will need to convince others, most commonly the high street banks, that you are a 'good risk' from their point of view.

After the problems associated with high levels of borrowing which many small business owners experienced in the 1980s, there is a growing tendency now for many individuals starting up in business to try to avoid the use of external sources of finance. This may not be practical or possible in your case, but it might be worth considering whether, say, members of your family are prepared to offer financial support, particularly if the sums involved are not too great.

The only way to assess your finance requirement is to prepare cashflow and profit projections – even if you have little or no experience in this type of exercise. The preparation of projections is covered in detail in chapter 3.

Do you have the necessary personal qualities and support?

To have any chance of making a success of your business, you will have to be absolutely committed to it. You will need determination and stamina, and you will have to learn to cope with levels of stress which are not generally experienced as an employee. You may have worked previously in a fast-moving, demanding work environment and be accustomed to shouldering responsibility for important projects. While this is all good experience, it is simply not the same as taking sole responsibility for your own business and its ultimate success or failure.

DO YOU HAVE THE TEMPERAMENT?

Think carefully before getting started whether you have the temperament to run your own business. If you like an easy-going, stress-free life where you can switch off thoughts of your job at 5.30, then you should consider seriously whether you are temperamentally suited to being in charge of your own business. If you are planning to work entirely on your own, there may be some scope for flexibility, although you will still be completely at the beck and call of your clients or customers. If you had planned a day off and a client contacts you with a problem, for example, nobody else will be able to cover for you. You will have to accept some disruption of your personal and social life as a normal hazard of running your own business.

DO YOU HAVE THE DETERMINATION?

You will need great determination to succeed. For some people this may be a natural quality, but if not you will have to develop perseverence and mental strength. You are not a robot and there will be occasions when you feel uncertain or dejected, or simply wish you had never started the business. It is helpful to have friends or business associates working in similar circumstances (but not in competition with you) whom you can trust and confide in at these moments. You will probably find they have had similar if not worse experiences and can offer valuable support when you feel at a low ebb. You may be tempted never to admit to problems: perhaps you feel it will detract from the image you want to create of yourself as a successful businessperson within the local business community. However, be realistic: you will need to have an outlet outside your family for your problems and doubts.

An accountant who set up his own sole practice after spending some years working for a large firm found this type of support invaluable. A former colleague had set up a very similar practice at roughly the same time in a different part of the country. Because their situations were so similar, they were able to draw on each other's experiences and technical knowledge for support. Some five years later, they continue to talk regularly on the phone, not only for technical consultation but also for moral support at times when either feels low about a particular situation or the business in general. They are both happy to admit that they find this support vital, and without it would find running their practices much more stressful.

DO YOU HAVE SUPPORT?

Quite apart from your own personal qualities, you will need the committed support of your spouse or partner and family. If they are actively against your wish to start your own business, consider their reasons. Are they afraid that it will require all of your time? Do they fear the financial insecurity of losing a regular income? Do they feel that you are temperamentally unsuited to running a business? It can be helpful if these reasons are written down, to provide a basis for rational discussion, otherwise it is easy for discussion to become unfocused. Equally, discuss with them the reasons why you want to start your own business.

Getting the business started will be more difficult, especially in the early stages, if you do not have the active encouragement of your family. There may be resentment, and strained relations may result from the time and energy you have to put into your business. On the other hand, with their support, you may be able to benefit not only from practical help but also from sharing problems and decision-making. Your family may ultimately find it surprisingly rewarding and satisfying.

However much careful consideration and planning goes into the decision to start a business, nobody can know exactly what it will be like until the business is underway. In spite of this, good research, discussion and thought beforehand will mean that you are at least aware of some of the hazards and problems you will be facing. Remember that you are the best person to assess your suitability for starting your own business, and you will need to be ruthlessly honest with yourself in your self-assessment.

2 **Before you start trading**

If you have thought about the more general aspects of being in business on your own and have decided that you want to proceed with your business idea, you now need to move on to more specific issues.

It is essential *before* proceeding to set up your business to carry out some thorough research into how it is going to work, however simple you expect its operation to be. While doing this research, you may come across factors that adversely affect your decision to start the business: for example, a direct competitor who has recently and successfully become established locally will make your plans much less feasible. If you begin to have doubts or simply decide that being in business on your own is not what you want, do not be afraid either to postpone or to abandon your plans. You will never make a success of your business if you feel half-hearted about the idea: it will demand your complete commitment if you are to have any chance of success.

Some of the issues you will have to consider will be specific to your own business; others will be more general. They will include:

- market research;
- estimates of financial viability;
- deciding on the most appropriate trading entity;
- consulting professionals and specialists;
- organizing training courses.

Market research

Setting up a business on the assumption that individuals or other businesses will want to purchase your product or service is probably a fast route to failure. While your business is still at the planning stage, it is vital to assess your potential market and judge whether you can generate sufficient sales to make the business feasible. There is no point in creating a miraculous new product if you are unable to sell it. Similarly, if you are operating in a very specialist market, you need to ensure that sufficient demand exists for your service.

A musician developed his skills as a repairer of violins and other stringed instruments, having decided that making a living as a professional musician was no longer possible for him. He was located in a small and fairly remote village, and had assumed that friends, contacts and local advertising would provide him with sufficient work to make a reasonable living. However, he had overestimated the demand for his skills, and although he enjoyed his work it simply did not provide him with sufficient income to cover even his basic expenses. He was fortunate in having the skills to offer music tuition to supplement his income, otherwise he feels he would have been forced to abandon his business.

You need to consider the following questions.

- What product or service are you offering?
- How will you reach your target market?
- What is the state of the market sector and who are your competitors?
- How will you create an identity for your product or service?

What product or service are you offering?

First, you have to sell a product or service for which there is a demand. You may believe that the electric car you have designed will capture the imagination of consumers and make you a millionaire, but you must be realistic and objective about your chances of succeeding where others have already failed. It is easier to sell a product for which there is already an acknowledged need than to persuade potential customers of the need for a new product.

If you are manufacturing a product, are you sure that you are offering your customers what they want? You should compare your product with alternative ones already on the market, and try to consider ways in which yours can improve on those alternatives. What range of products will you be able to offer? Will your customers expect a choice, or will they be satisfied with a single 'base' product? If there is a long lead time (the time taken between the customer's order and the delivery of the product), will this be acceptable or will potential customers try elsewhere? Will you be able to offer a maintenance or repair service, if this is appropriate?

If you are a retailer, you will have to decide on the types of goods you think will appeal most to your customers and will encourage them to return to your shop in preference to others. A small general store might aim to stock a wide range of goods at competitive prices, for example. It might also have longer opening hours than local competitors, or open on a Sunday to encourage extra trade. A clothes shop situated in a prosperous area might decide to create an up-market image, with a relatively small number of high quality, more expensive lines. A bookshop could try to cater primarily for the needs of students at the local college, by liaising with staff to ascertain the texts on students' reading lists in advance of the beginning of each term.

If you are providing a service, you will need to define exactly what areas that service covers. If you are a despatch rider, is there a limit to the distance you are prepared to drive for your customers? As a decorator, are you also able to carry out building work, or is it beyond your training and experience? If you are offering training or coaching services, to what level are you able to teach your clients or students? You need to decide in advance how limited or extensive a service you are able to provide. It is often tempting to offer a more extensive service than you are able to deliver – and to lose potential repeat customers as a result. Be aware of your limitations, whether they are self-imposed or otherwise, and be honest with your customers.

A computer consultant set up a business providing general hardware and software support to clients. He judged that small businesses in particular often do not have an in-house computer specialist, and perceived that many would welcome a general support service. His experience and contacts were sufficient to get the business off the ground, the bulk of his work involving *ad hoc* projects and on-going support to a growing nucleus of clients, whom he charged a standard monthly fee for this type of work. He was guaranteed a reasonable monthly income, and his clients enjoyed the benefit of an expert who was usually able to visit them the same or the next day when required. He had judged the market accurately and worked hard to increase his client base, creating a profitable and secure business.

How will you reach your target market?

Your product or service will, to a certain extent, define your market. A large, multi-national company is unlikely to use the services of a self-employed electrician working alone. Conversely, an individual consumer will not usually be interested in industrial cleaning services. You will need to devise forms of advertising your product or service which are appropriate to your business: there is little point in a local solicitor advertising in a national newspaper.

If you are intending to operate mainly in a local market, advertising regularly in the 'Classified' section of local newspapers, or buying advertising space on the editorial pages, is a reasonably cheap means of reaching a large local market, as is advertising in the *Yellow Pages*. You might also try sending a mailshot to local businesses which might have a need for your product or service. If possible, try to obtain the name of the appropriate person within the organization to address your letter to. Do be aware, however, that the success rate for this type of advertising is extremely low. Local business contacts are also likely to be valuable in introducing you to potential customers or clients, particularly once the business is underway and your network of contacts starts to grow.

If you intend to operate on a broader geographical scale, you will find trade journals, organizations or exhibitions useful as sources of information. Try looking in your local library for publications such as the *Directory of British Associations*. If you can attend trade shows and talk to businesses which are already operating in your sector, you may be able to get hold of promotional literature and general information about the products or services already on the market.

What is the state of the market sector and who are your competitors?

If you are working in a market sector with which you are already familiar, you will probably have a reasonable idea of whether it is growing or shrinking, how much it is affected by economic trends, and so on. If you are less familiar with the market, consulting trade journals should help to provide you with good general information and background. For example, you may discover from articles or the Classified Advertisements section that competition in your market sector is particularly strong, and that you will need to devise a means of giving your product the edge over those of your competitors. Alternatively, you may find that a useful gap in the market exists, which you have the skills and knowledge to exploit.

If you are operating a retail business, it may be appropriate for you to look at your market at a more local level. If you plan to open an antiques shop, for example, is it preferable to locate your business in a small town where similar shops already exist, or in a neighbouring town where you have no direct competition? In the first case, you have the advantage of attracting chance customers who intended to visit your competitors; in the second, you have the advantage of no immediate local competition.

On the other hand, if you are setting up, say, a hairdressing business in a village where one already exists, you may have problems attracting sufficient customers from a fairly small population. Perhaps you might achieve better results if you are prepared to offer a mobile service which covers a larger geographical area.

How will you create an identity for your product or service?

It can be difficult both to introduce a new product or service and to try to compete in an established market. In the first case, you have the disadvantage of trying to convince your potential market that they need your product. In the latter case, you may have to try to create a niche in the market or target a particular sector because there are already alternatives available.

There are various ways of creating a particular identity for your business, or, specifically, for your product or service. You can emphasize features such as:

- price;
- quality/reliability;
- speed of delivery;
- quality of client/customer relations;
- professionalism.

You might decide, for example, that although you cannot match the prices offered by your local competitor, you can supply a better quality product or service with a faster delivery time, or a similar quality product with a guaranteed next-day delivery. You will have to emphasize these factors when you are approached by potential customers and convince them that your product or service is better than the available alternatives.

Once you have decided on the identity that you want to create for your business, you must ensure that you are able to live up to your aims. If you claim that your product will last for five years, your reputation will quickly begin to suffer if it consistently wears out after eighteen months. Similarly, do not offer an emergency 24-hour call-out service unless you have the staff available to provide it.

Try to put yourself in the position of your clients or customers and ask yourself which factors would be most important to you. In some cases, price will be critical. In others, reliability or the availability of a maintenance service might be of far greater significance.

Although it will inevitably take some time for your identity to become established, do persevere. The cheerful service engineer who always arrives in a clean van and clean overalls *does* make a favourable impression, however trivial these details might seem.

A farmer built up a successful farm shop selling organically grown fruit and vegetables, after becoming aware of the growing popularity of this type of produce. There was no similar shop in the immediate area. He started on a very small scale by delivering to a small number of customers. As demand grew, he felt it was worthwhile to open a shop to attract a larger volume of customers, although he continued to offer a home delivery service. He admits that it did take some time to establish his reputation, but by ensuring that his produce was always fresh and sufficiently competitive in price, he now has a useful addition to his farming business.

Estimates of financial viability

Preparing financial projections and a business plan and deciding on suitable sources of finance are covered in detail in chapter 3, but at this stage it is useful to make some rough estimates of financial performance. Your business proposition may not be financially viable; this is the time to make that discovery, rather than in a year's time when you are unable to meet your financial commitments.

Although you may have difficulty estimating what level of sales you can make, you can probably estimate some of your costs reasonably accurately. Once you have determined your total costs and the level of profit you aim to make, you can work out the level of sales you require in order to cover those costs and profit.

How will you obtain the information you need to estimate your overheads and costs? Some items may need research. You can:

- ask local estate agents about office rents;
- check with business directories, newspapers or journals about their advertising rates;
- contact your insurance broker about likely levels of motor, office and other forms of insurance;
- request information about salary rates from recruitment agencies;
- ask local accountants and solicitors for rough estimates of costs for the first year;
- investigate the costs of producing letterheads, business cards, invoices etc. with local printers.

This may sound difficult and time-consuming, but much of the information can probably be obtained by means of a few phone calls. Other items, such as phone and fax running costs, postage and travel and subsistence (meals, hotel bills etc. when you are working away from the office) may have to take the form of an educated guess.

A graphic designer plans to leave her current employment and set up in business on her own. She estimates her overheads and the amount of money she will need to draw out of the business for herself for the first year, adds her desired profit and thereby calculates the level of fees she needs to bill to clients to make her business financially viable. At this stage, she takes no account of Value Added Tax in her calculations.

Net drawings for self	15,000
Taxation/National Insurance estimate	5,000
Office rent and rates	4,000
Heat and light	400
Telephone and fax	1,200
Materials	2,500
Postage and stationery	600
Admin. salary (part-time)	6,000
Motor expenses	2,500
Insurance	1,000
Books and publications	500
Advertising	500
Travel and subsistence	600
Legal and professional costs	1,500
Bank charges	400
Sundry expenses (contingency)	1,200

Total overheads	42,900
Desired profit at year end	10,000
Minimum fees required	£52,900

In her current job, she generates in the region of £80,000 of fees a year. She knows that two of her major clients will remain loyal to her when she leaves her employment, and feels she will be able to generate sufficient additional work to achieve a turnover of at least £52,900.

Her calculations are not detailed or complicated, but they do give her the assurance that her planned business enterprise is worth pursuing. If, on the other hand, her calculations had indicated a need to bill, say, £85,000 to clients in her first year, she would have to re-examine her costs and overheads to see if these could be reduced. If not, she would have to think seriously about the risk she was taking in setting up her own business.

This type of analysis is fairly rough and ready: it will not be sufficiently detailed to enable you to work out how much finance you will require to get your business started, for example. However, it is useful as a starting-point, and will help you to start to focus on the information you will need to prepare more detailed financial projections, which are discussed in chapter 3.

Trading entities

Before you start to trade, you must decide upon the most appropriate legal form for your trading entity. The three most common forms are:

- sole trader
- partnership
- limited company.

There are various considerations which can help you to reach your decision, and it is a good idea to consult an accountant or other professional adviser in case there are issues specific to your particular business which might affect your choice. It is easier (and potentially much cheaper) to spend some time considering the options now, than to change your mind later on. Sorting out in your own mind the differences between the three types of trading entity and which is most suitable for your business may seem daunting, particularly if there are unfamiliar concepts and jargon. However, this is not a good reason to duck the issue: it is important to make a decision which is right for your business.

Sole trader

Although the term 'sole trader' implies that you work alone, it actually refers to the fact that you, as proprietor, take all responsibility for the liabilities of the business. If the business itself is unable to meet its financial obligations, then creditors may seek financial recourse from you personally.

It is very easy to start up in business as a sole trader, by informing your local tax office and DSS office that you are becoming self-employed, and contacting your local VAT office, if necessary, to arrange to register for VAT purposes (see chapter 6).

You will have to prepare accounts for your business for tax purposes, in order to compute the income tax and Class 4 National Insurance contributions due on the profits you make, or if you make losses, to compute your tax losses. Your accounts will not be subject to any form of audit, and your tax will be calculated at the rates of income tax in force at that time.

If you make tax losses, then you will be able to offset these against future profits from the same trade, or from any other income you may have in the relevant period. Similarly, it is possible to carry back tax losses for a period of three years to offset against income in those years.

You will probably also have to pay Class 2 National Insurance contributions (formerly known as the 'stamp'), unless you are earning beneath the 'Lower Earnings Limit'. You have to apply for exemption from Class 2 contributions in this case, so discuss it with your professional adviser if you think it will apply to you.

Partnership

A partnership is also easy to set up. It refers to two or more individuals who trade in business together, each taking a share of the profits. It is extremely important to have a legal partnership deed drawn up by a solicitor, even if it is a simple family partnership. The deed does not need to be long or complex, but it should set out:

- the name of the business and its trading activity;
- the names of the partners;
- the date the partnership is to commence and how long it is to last;
- the profit-sharing ratios;
- the rights of the partners should one wish to leave, retire or sell his or her interest, or on death of a partner;
- details of arbitration procedures should there be a breakdown in 'goodwill' between the partners.

It may also be useful to include:

- details of holiday entitlements, where appropriate;
- details of responsibility for management of the business.

Particularly where the partnership involves members of a family, or good friends or colleagues who have worked together previously, some of these details may not seem necessary. However, family and working relationships can change or break down, so it is advisable to incorporate these matters in the deed by mutual agreement at the outset. For similar reasons, where just two partners are involved, a 50:50 partnership is not always a good idea: a position of stalemate can be reached if goodwill breaks down. If arbitration procedures have been set out in the partnership deed, this may not be an insurmountable problem.

Deciding on the profit-sharing ratios is a matter to be decided between the partners: there is no formula for reaching this decision. However, some of the factors you might take into account include:

- the roles played by each of the partners in the business;
- the time committed by each partner to the business;
- the skills and resources introduced into the business by each partner.

It may be that these are all roughly similar for each partner, but that one of the (say) three will clearly be the driving force behind the business. The partnership might be structured so that this partner has a slightly larger share – such as 40 per cent, compared with 30 per cent for the other two partners. If just two partners were involved, maybe a 45 per cent to 55 per cent split might be appropriate, or possibly 49 per cent to 51 per cent. In another case, one of two partners might play a very minor role in the business, and the ratios could be adjusted accordingly.

If you and your partner(s) are unable to agree on the ratios, perhaps you should consider whether the future running of the business will be fraught with the same problems. The same applies to decisions about how much money the partners are expected to put into the business and how much they are entitled to draw from it.

As with a sole trader, the liabilities of the partners are unlimited. Additionally, each partner is responsible for the other partners' share of the debts ('joint and several liability'). This means that if one partner defaults on the payment of liabilities, then creditors have recourse to the other partners. The partnership has to prepare accounts, although they do not require an audit. The partners' income tax and Class 4 National Insurance liabilities will be based on the profits shown by the accounts, in their profit-sharing ratios. The rate of tax on the profits depends on the tax rates applicable to the individual partners on their income. It may be possible to use tax losses advantageously.

The partners are also likely to pay Class 2 National Insurance contributions (see 'Sole trader' above).

Limited company

Under normal circumstances, the liability of a shareholder in a limited company is restricted. However, it is often the case with new and small companies that bankers and suppliers ask for personal guarantees from the directors – who are often also the shareholders – before lending money or supplying goods or services. If the company is unable to meet its financial commitments, creditors may turn to the provider of the guarantees for payment.

The regulations for the preparation and audit of accounts are more stringent than for either a sole trader or a partnership. A limited company has to file statutory accounts in a prescribed format at Companies House, and, depending upon the size and type of the company and the wishes of the shareholders, they may be subject to an audit. An audit involves not only the preparation of accounts from your books and records, but also an examination of the underlying documents (invoices, bank statements, cheque books, VAT returns, wages records, stock records and so on) to make sure they support the figures in your books and therefore in the accounts. Theoretically, the purpose of the audit is to provide assurance to external shareholders that the accounts show 'a true and fair view' of the company's results for the period in question. The accounts filed at Companies House are available for examination by the public.

As a director of the company, you will also be an employee and the company will have to set up and administer a PAYE scheme. Under the scheme, deductions of PAYE and National Insurance have to be made from the salary ('director's remuneration') which you are paid. These deductions are usually paid to the Inland Revenue monthly. More details on the administration of a PAYE scheme are included in chapter 6. As well as the income tax deducted from your director's remuneration, the company will also pay Corporation Tax on its retained profits.

There are also specific responsibilities that apply to directors of limited companies, which broadly cover acting in good faith for the company, with proper regard for the interests of shareholders and employees, not knowingly allowing the company to trade while insolvent, not carrying on business with intent to defraud, and compliance with the requirements of the Companies Act. Additionally, if a company trades fraudulently or is guilty of wrongful trading (knowingly trading while insolvent), then directors may become personally liable for its liabilities. They can also be disqualified from being company directors for up to fifteen years.

It is more costly to set up a limited company, and there are two ways of doing so. In either case, you will need the assistance of your professional adviser to ensure that all the necessary details are filed at Companies House. You can set up a brand new company, or you can buy a ready-made one 'off the shelf' and change its name, details of directors, shareholders and so on. A company must have at least one director, a company secretary (who may not also be the sole director) and at least two shareholders.

Advantages and disadvantages of trading entities

ADVANTAGES OF SOLE TRADER/PARTNERSHIP

- Ease of formation.
- No public right of access to accounts, so confidentiality can be maintained.
- No legal audit requirement.
- PAYE and National Insurance do not need to be paid at the time the sole trader/partner draws cash out of the business. There may therefore be a timing advantage in the payment of income tax and National Insurance.
- The business can be incorporated as a limited company at a later date, if required (subject to consideration of the taxation implications).

DISADVANTAGES OF SOLE TRADER/PARTNERSHIP

- May have less credibility: customers, suppliers and financiers may feel, perhaps irrationally, more comfortable dealing with a limited company.

- Transferring ownership to future generations in a partnership can be difficult.
- Unlimited financial liability.
- Income tax and National Insurance are payable on profits, *not* cash drawings. Potentially, retained profits can be taxed more heavily than in a limited company.

ADVANTAGES OF LIMITED COMPANY

- May have greater credibility with customers, suppliers and bankers.
- The liabilities of the directors are limited, subject to personal guarantees.
- Income tax is payable on salaries drawn. High personal tax rates might be avoided if profits are retained in the business and become subject to Corporation Tax.
- Greater flexibility to make pension contributions.
- Ownership can be transferred or extended relatively easily through the issue or transfer of shares.

DISADVANTAGES OF LIMITED COMPANY

- Disclosure of information to the public.
- Potential legal audit requirement.
- Prohibition on loans from the company to directors.
- Compliance with the Companies Act required.
- Operation of PAYE and National Insurance regulations on all remuneration and benefits, including, for example, cars and fuel.
- Potentially double charge to tax on capital gains (when you sell the asset and when you take the proceeds out of the company).
- Potential requirement to provide personal guarantees undermines the attractive concept of limited liability.
- The Insolvency Act and the Disqualification of Directors Act impose severe penalties for transgressions.

You may already have strong ideas about the most appropriate trading entity for your business. Alternatively, you may be constrained by the fact that a potential customer or client has reasons for preferring to deal with a limited company rather than a sole trader or partnership. In general, it is far easier to convert a business later from a sole trader or a partnership to a limited company than vice versa.

It is worth emphasizing that although you may be more concerned with how to win sales than with the technicalities of choosing the right trading entity, it is important to make the right choice. Remember that it is a matter you should have to confront only once.

A former marketing executive set up a business organizing corporate hospitality. It was to be run on a small scale, with two other individuals. It was decided to set up a group of five limited companies – one holding company and four subsidiaries. The trading operations in each of the subsidiary companies were to be identical. The apparent rationale for setting up five separate companies was that each would handle contracts with different corporate clients, although there seemed to be no sound reason why this was necessary. The business did not perform well. The directors – who were also the shareholders – had already suffered the administrative nightmare of trying to manage four separate trading entities, and soon discovered the professional costs for doing so were out of all proportion to the size of the business overall. When the business ceased trading, the cost of winding up the companies was, again, enormous. Even now, they are unable to explain why they set up such a complicated structure, and regret not discussing it with a number of different advisers who might have provided simpler solutions.

Professional and specialist advice

Consulting the right adviser at the right time and drawing on their specialist knowledge can save you considerable time and energy in reaching decisions about the formation and running of your business. The advisers you are most likely to need in the early stages include:

- solicitor
- accountant
- banker

In all cases, do 'shop around' and ask business associates for their personal recommendations. Where appropriate, take up references or carry out other checks to ensure that individuals or firms belong to the relevant professional body. Your aim is to establish productive and, in some cases, long-term working relationships with these advisers, so you need to feel confident that you are able to work together satisfactorily and that factors such as a clash of personalities will not cloud that relationship.

Where you will be paying fees for their services, do not let price alone influence your choice of adviser. In the initial stages of setting up your business when you are trying to keep your costs at a reasonable level, it can be tempting to settle for the cheapest quote. Obviously, cost has to be a consideration, but if you are offered three price quotes in the region of £1,000 and one of £500, do not necessarily assume that you will receive the same quality of service at the cheapest price.

Training

Training falls into two categories:

- general business training;
- specific technical/specialist training relevant to your particular business.

General business training

There is some debate about the benefits of business training and whether it can help to contribute to the success or failure of your business. It has been argued that participants in some business start-up training courses were as likely to fail in their business as non-participants. It could however be that these businesses would have failed in any case and that the training courses were not a factor.

If you feel it would be helpful or if you know that you lack experience in particular areas, it is probably worthwhile investigating courses run either by your local Training and Enterprise Council or by private firms or training agencies. Training courses can certainly help to fill gaps in your knowledge or experience, but beware the temptation to think that you can become an expert in anything after a two-day training course.

> An experienced picture-framer decided to set up his own framing business, and looked for suitable general business training courses before leaving his job. He attended a three-day course which gave a basic grounding in business management, but felt baffled and confused by the end of the course. A variety of areas had been covered, but none in the depth he felt he needed. He realized he needed more guidance and looked around for separate specialist courses on marketing, finance and so on. He attended these over a period of months, so that he could absorb gradually the information he needed to manage his business effectively. Several years on, he has been proved right and has a successful and stable business which provides him with a more than adequate income.

The time to think about this type of training is ideally before the business is up and running. Once the business gets started, there are likely to be far greater pressures on your time, and training will not be your first priority. You should also consider whether you want to attend full-time or part-time courses, whether you prefer a block of training of, say, four weeks or a number of sessions spread over several months or a year. You should also think about the areas in which you most need training. For example:

- general business management
- accounting and finance
- preparing a business plan
- marketing
- selling
- being an employer
- management skills.

A pig breeder specializing in rare and fine pig breeds found that marketing training helped him to identify and sell to customers in ways he had not previously considered. He had started by offering joints of pork only, selling to individual consumers in units of half a pig. He began to build a reputation for the high quality of his meat, but had difficulty increasing his customer base. After taking part in a marketing course and talking to his existing customers, he decided to pursue two strategies. The first was to offer a wider range of products, including bacon and assorted varieties of sausages. The second was to approach up-market hotels and restaurants, as a means of breaking into a different market. Both were more productive than he had anticipated: sales of sausages and bacon were an immediate success, bringing a large number of new customers. Sales to hotels and restaurants were more limited, but with hard work, perseverance and flexibility, he managed to secure a regular purchase from an extremely prestigious local restaurant, which helped to boost his reputation still further.

He strongly recommends new business owners to recognize the areas in which they lack expertise, and to take action to improve their skills. For his business, it has led to a significant increase in turnover and profits, at a time when he had been wondering whether to continue with the business at all.

Specific technical/specialist training

It may be important in your particular business sector for you to keep your technical or specialist knowledge and skills up to date, particularly if they are periodically subject to legislative, scientific or technological change, for example.

If this is the case, your clients or customers will justifiably expect you to keep abreast of developments and changes in your field. You may have previously worked within a larger organization where training was provided for you to ensure that your skills were kept up to date. You will probably be able to gain a certain amount of information from technical journals, but you should not rely entirely on these. Good intentions of reading important articles can easily be overtaken by more urgent tasks and never come to fruition. In spite of the extra cost, you may find it more effective in the longer term to attend specialist training courses, organized either by professional bodies or by private firms. These can also be useful for making new contacts in your business field.

3 Preparing a business plan and raising finance

Whatever your business, you will want to know – before you start – how much finance you need for start-up costs and to provide working capital. The amount you require will depend largely on the type and scale of the business you are setting up: a music teacher working from home will obviously need less than a manufacturer of office furniture, or a bookshop.

You may be able to provide sufficient cash yourself to get your business started and to provide adequate working capital in the early stages, or you may need to seek additional finance from external sources. The source you choose will probably depend on the level of finance you need to raise; if a relatively small bank overdraft will suffice, then it is unlikely to be worthwhile approaching venture capitalists.

If you have done any research into your prospective business, you will already have some idea of both the start-up and on-going costs you expect to incur, such as:

- purchase of manufacturing or office equipment;
- office rent;
- salaries;
- cost of goods for resale.

You may also have a rough idea of the level of sales you think you could achieve, and of sales prices or charge-out rates. On the other hand, you may have done little or no research, but believe that you can generate sufficient sales or turnover to make your business profitable and generate a positive cashflow almost immediately.

In either case, you won't yet have a really clear idea of how profitable your business will be or how much cash it will generate. Obviously, you will want to assess how you expect the business to perform and how much finance you require. This can really only be done properly by preparing cash and profit projections, in a form as simple or as sophisticated as is appropriate for your particular business. If you have spent some time thinking about your business idea, you will already know how tricky it is to judge how well it will perform.

In any case, any external providers of finance you approach will want to look at your cash and profit projections and business plan in order to establish whether you are a suitable risk as a borrower. Some banks and other institutions will provide you with pro-forma cash and profit projection forms to fill in. However, if you intend to approach several banks or institutions, it is generally easier to prepare one set of projections which you can present to various potential lenders, rather than to fill in a number of different forms.

The proprietor of a newly re-established nursery discovered that he had badly misjudged his business's performance in its early stages and underestimated his finance requirement. Although he had spent some time trying to assess it before he set up the business, he had not incorporated his various calculations into formal projections. The business had previously been run by his mother on premises adjoining his parents' farm, but she had wound it up several years previously because of other pressures on her time. His initial outlay for improving the premises was not that great and he was able to finance this expenditure from his own savings, carrying out most of the work himself. However, he had not fully taken into account the time required for the plants he was raising to mature to a point where they were saleable. Additionally, he had underestimated the effects of disease and other factors which would reduce his stock. Although he had budgeted for the purchase of a certain level of stock from other sources, he found that he was forced to spend considerably more than he had anticipated in order to offer sufficient variety and quantity to his customers. He had hoped to manage without resorting to any external borrowing, but was soon forced to approach his bankers for an overdraft facility.

Clearly, the practical problems he experienced would have occurred even if he had paid more attention to his projected financial performance. However, his financial problems could have been planned for if he had devoted more attention to his monthly sales and costs, and the timing of the cashflow in and out of the business.

Although your projections will focus on the financial aspects of your business, they will necessarily highlight more general issues.

- How will you win the orders or custom to generate your projected level of sales?
- Are you sure that you can employ the staff you want at the salaries you are prepared to pay?
- Do you know that the premises you have budgeted for are available?

Do not think of preparing your projections as a purely financial exercise. Think of it as a jigsaw, where you look at all the different elements of your business and work out how they will all slot together to make a coherent whole. Use it as an opportunity to do some general planning, and spend time thinking about exactly how your business is going to work.

You may prefer to ask an accountant to help you to formulate your financial projections. However, do not forget that you will still have to provide all the information which makes up the projections, so it is still worth spending time working through all the details that will be required.

Financial projections

For a brand new business, it is not easy to forecast with any certainty some of the elements in its financial projections. You have no past records to use as a guide, and you might feel initially that any attempt to predict future performance is no more than a stab in the dark. However, once you have done some groundwork, you will find that there are certain figures that you do know in advance, and others that you can estimate with reasonable accuracy. For the figures which are very uncertain – and sales often falls into this category – ensure that you have some basis for your estimate. When you present your case for finance you will be asked to explain and justify your figures, so there is no point in simply plucking a round sum out of the air and hoping it will suffice.

You will need to prepare both a profit projection and a cashflow projection. It is important to be clear about the distinction between the two and why they are both needed. A profit projection sets out your estimate of sales for a given period (regardless of when you actually receive payment), together with the costs and expenses which relate to those sales – materials, labour, overheads and so on. You can then arrive at the profit or loss for that trading period.

It is extremely unlikely that you will receive payment for every sale as soon as it is made, nor pay for all your purchases and expenses as soon as they are incurred. You may well have credit arrangements with customers and/ or suppliers. The amount of profit you expect to make will not be the same as the amount of cash you have in the bank, because there are timing differences between when a transaction occurs and when payment is made or received. Additionally, there are items which figure in the profit projection but not in the cashflow, such as depreciation of fixed assets, and items which figure in the cashflow forecast but not in the profit projection, such as payments of VAT to HM Customs and Excise. You therefore need to estimate when you will pay out or receive cash and to translate this into a cashflow projection.

Although your cash position is probably the issue which will concern you most at this stage, it is advisable to start with your profit projection. It is extremely difficult to predict when you will receive or pay out cash until you have estimated your levels of sales and costs.

If you have a reasonable working knowledge of spreadsheet software, it is ideal for preparing financial projections. Unlike manual calculations, you are able to change or add figures and the spreadsheet will automatically rework any calculations which have been affected. This both saves time, and should help to eliminate arithmetical errors. However, if you are not familiar with spreadsheets or do not have access to a computer, you can prepare projections manually: the principles are exactly the same.

Projected profit and loss account

Your projected profit and loss account, as the name suggests, is where you estimate how much profit or loss your business will make. To do this, you need to work out the level of sales you hope to make in a given period and subtract from that the direct costs and overheads which relate to that same period. While reading this section you may find it helpful to refer to the illustrative projections for ABC Office Services later in this chapter, to get an idea of how your plan might look when it is completed.

As you work through your projections, make notes of your assumptions about sales and costs. These will form an important part of your projections, so that a reader can understand how you have arrived at your figures. For example, if your sales are seasonal and will peak in the summer, explain this. Similarly, if you expect to build up steadily month by month in the first twelve months, explain in your plan how you expect to achieve this.

Sales

The first figure you will try to work out is your sales, which is often one of the most difficult to estimate, whether you are selling a product or a service.

If you are selling a product, estimate how many units you expect to sell each week or month, and multiply that figure by your anticipated selling price. If you are selling a service, try to calculate your sales by working out the number of clients you expect to gain and the fees you anticipate charging them. Some people prefer to make an estimate for, say, the first twelve months and simply divide that number by twelve to achieve their monthly sales. However, this will not be realistic for the vast majority of businesses. Even in retail businesses where sales are not expected to fluctuate unduly, it is unlikely that the level of sales achieved in month one will be the same as that in month six or month twelve. Do think about seasonal fluctuations and other factors, such as your plans for developing your customer or client base.

Remember that unless you are running a business in which all of your customers pay you immediately by cash or cheque etc., you are not interested at this stage in the amounts or timing of cash received. The figures you need are for the level of sales you expect to make to customers or clients in the period, regardless of when they are paid.

If you are registered for VAT, do not include VAT in your sales figures.

Once you are happy that you have a reasonable monthly estimate for your sales, enter these figures in the first line of your profit projection.

Cost of sales

The next item to calculate is your 'cost of sales'. This refers to the costs which are directly attributable to the sales of your product or service. Unlike some of your overheads, such as rent, which will have to be paid whether the business makes any sales or not, these costs will generally increase or decrease according to your level of sales.

For a manufacturer, this will include the purchases of materials and so on which go into making up the product; for a decorator, electrician, plumber etc., it will include the materials purchased for customers; for a retail business, it will be the goods purchased for resale to customers. If you are selling a service which basically entails selling your time to clients, then your cost of sales is likely to be small, perhaps comprising only the expenses you incur and subsequently recharge to clients (known as 'disbursements'), such as travel costs. Again, these costs should be entered in your profit projection net of VAT if you intend to become VAT registered.

In some cases, you may find that you can work out your cost of sales as a percentage of your sales. For example, if you have calculated that the cost of manufacturing your product is £40 and you decide you can sell it for £80, then your cost of goods is 50 per cent of the selling price.

If you are manufacturing a product, you will also include in your cost of sales the labour cost which has gone into the manufacturing process. If, for example, the wages of two employees are directly attributable to that manufacturing process, then they will be incorporated in your cost of sales.

When you have worked out your cost of sales for each month, enter these figures in the next line of your profit projection, below the figures for sales. If you have several different types of cost of sales, such as goods and wages, enter these on separate lines, so that your projection is as clear as possible. Again, if you intend to register for VAT, enter these figures net of VAT, where appropriate.

Gross profit

Gross profit is the difference between sales and cost of sales. To calculate your gross profit, subtract your cost of sales figure from your sales figure, and enter this on the next line down.

As well as calculating the monetary value of gross profit, it is also useful to calculate it as a percentage which you can use as a guide to highlight any unusual monthly fluctuations. The percentage is calculated as

$$\frac{\text{Gross profit} \times 100}{\text{Sales}} = \text{gross profit percentage}$$

From the example above, the gross profit percentage would be 50 per cent, calculated as

$$\frac{40 \times 100}{80} = 50 \text{ per cent}$$

If possible, it is also useful to compare your own gross percentage with that of businesses in the same market field.

Overheads

Next you come to your estimates for overheads. Your own overheads will depend to some extent on the type of business you are running, whether you have employees, premises and so on. It is obviously not possible to compile a definitive list of every single overhead, but the list below includes some suggestions grouped together under their appropriate headings.

Distribution costs
> Transport
> Storage

Property costs
> Rent
> Business rates/water rates
> Electricity/gas
> Insurance
> Service charge
> Maintenance/repairs

Administration costs
> Wages and salaries, plus employer's National Insurance
> Director's remuneration plus National Insurance (limited companies only)
> Printing, postage and stationery
> Advertising and marketing

Motor costs – petrol, maintenance, Road Fund Licence, insurance
Computer maintenance and supplies
Operating leases
Subscriptions
Books and publications
Training
Office/other business insurance
Repairs and renewals
Travel
Subsistence
Entertaining
Sundry expenses

Professional costs
Legal
Accountancy/audit

Finance costs
Bank charges
Bank current account interest
Loan interest
Hire purchase interest

Other costs
Bad debt charges
Depreciation
Profit/loss on disposal of fixed assets.

Many of these may not apply to your business, and there may be others which you should include. Make a list first, then try to estimate the cost of these items. You should be able to find out about some by means of phone calls to estate agents, insurance brokers, employment agencies and so on. Certain others will have to be estimated, which can be tricky, but you should be able to judge whether, say, your phone bill will be in the region of £100 or £1,000. Other items can be calculated. For example, you can find out what rates of interest banks are charging on overdrafts and loans and apply these to your figures.

Do not forget the one-off start-up costs which you will incur. These may be minimal if you intend to work from home, but may still include items such as:

- printing of stationery;
- advertising and publicity;
- legal and professional costs.

If you are purchasing premises, you may also need to pay for the installation of utilities and services, such as electricity or telephone lines.

Remember that in the profit projection you include the costs *incurred* by the business in the period, not the payments made. For example, if you estimate that your quarterly phone bill for May to July will be £300 excluding VAT, then the monthly charge for May, June and July is £100, regardless of when you actually pay the bill.

You may also find it useful to discuss your estimates with friends or associates who already have some experience of running a business. They may be able to provide you with a great deal of information, both financial and general.

As with your sales and costs of sales, if you intend to register for VAT, you will work out your figures for overheads net of VAT.

When you are happy with your list and estimates of overhead costs, enter these in your projection for each month beneath your gross profit. Add these up, to come to a total for your overheads.

Net profit

Subtract the total of your overheads from your gross profit to calculate your net profit (or loss) for each month. Remember that this is your projected profit before taxation.

Your profit projection will now look similar to the one for ABC Office Services below.

Cashflow projection

Next you should move on to your cashflow projection. In your cashflow projection, you estimate when you will receive and pay out money, based on the figures for sales and costs which you have entered in your profit projection. The purpose of the cashflow is to show you how your bank balance will fluctuate, and to help you to decide whether you need to arrange additional finance to support your business.

As you prepare your cashflow projection, make some brief notes about the assumptions you have used in deciding when you will receive payment for your sales and pay for your goods and expenses. Remember to include any VAT in the amounts you receive for your sales and in your payments wherever VAT is charged.

Again, you may find it helpful to refer to the illustrative cashflow for ABC Office Services for guidance.

Work through the cashflow projection line by line, as you did for your profit projection. Estimate first when you expect to receive payment for your sales, and enter this figure, including VAT if appropriate, since this is the amount you will actually receive from your customers.

On the next line, enter figures for any other money you expect to pay into your business bank account, such as capital which you introduce into the business. Add together these figures, to come to a total for bank receipts, and enter this on the line below.

Below your total bank receipts, list the costs and overheads which you entered in your profit projection and estimate when you will pay for these items – including VAT where appropriate. Some, such as travel costs, may be paid immediately. Others, such as telephone bills or insurance, may be paid quarterly or annually. Enter your figures in the appropriate month.

Next you need to think about any other payments you will make, for items which did not figure in your profit projection. These might include:

- purchases of equipment;
- your own drawings (sole trader and partnership only);
- VAT (to work out your VAT payments, see the description for ABC Office Services below).

When you have entered all your payments, add these together to come to a total for each month.

Subtract the total payments from the total receipts for the month to arrive at your net cash 'inflow' or 'outflow' for each month. Add this to the bank balance you started with at the beginning of the month to come to the bank balance at the end of each month.

You will now have a much clearer idea of how you expect your bank balance to fluctuate. The picture may be better than you expected, or more likely it may be worse. However, you are now no longer using pure guesswork, and are in a far stronger position to judge how much money you are going to require.

Judith is setting up ABC Office Services, providing administrative and marketing support to other businesses. She has previously worked in both large and small organizations, and has wide marketing experience and excellent administrative skills. She has already approached a number of small businesses, and gained some regular monthly work. Although she has some savings which she will use to cover her initial expenses, she wants to approach banks with a view to arranging an overdraft facility to cover the cash shortfalls which she anticipates may occur in her first year of trading. She is intending to register for VAT purposes, since she anticipates that her turnover will exceed the VAT threshold for compulsory registration (for more detail on VAT registration, see chapter 6).

She estimates that she will make sales of £2,250 excluding VAT in the first month, May 1995. She enters £2,250 in the projected profit and loss account for May 1995. She expects her sales to increase gradually through the year to £4,250 in April 1996. She enters these figures in the same way.

She then moves on to her projected cashflow to enter the figures for the cash she will actually receive from her customers, which will include VAT. She expects them to pay her 30 days after the invoice date. She works out that the cash she will receive for the sales she makes in May 1995 will amount to

Net sales	2,250.00
VAT @ 17.5%	393.75
Cash received from customers	£2,643.75

She rounds up this figure to the nearest £1, and enters £2,644 in the projected cashflow for June 1994, 30 days later.

The same principle applies to her expenses and overheads. She first makes a list of all the expenses she expects to incur, then tries to estimate what the costs will be. She enters these figures in the projected profit and loss account each month excluding VAT.

She then moves on to her projected cashflow, and works out when she expects to pay for those expenses. She enters these figures including VAT, where appropriate.

After entering all her estimates of payments for the expenses and overheads which she had included in her project projection, she now has to include any further payments for items which do not figure in the profit projection.

For example, if you intend to register for VAT, you will need to work out the estimated amount you will pay over to HM Customs and Excise each quarter, and enter this in your projected cashflow. Although there are many different regulations and complexities which govern the operation of VAT, the basic principle is a simple one.

First, work out the amount of VAT you have charged on your sales. Next work out the VAT which has been charged to you on your purchases, expenses and overheads. Now subtract the purchases VAT from the sales VAT. If your sales VAT is greater than the purchases VAT, you make a payment to Customs and Excise of the difference between the two. If the opposite is the case, you will receive a refund for that amount. Note that the payment (or refund) for the first three-month period is entered in the cashflow projection in month four, because this is the month in which you will actually pay over the money or receive the refund.

Judith also plans to purchase some office equipment and furniture. She has looked at both new and second-hand items, and come to a rough estimate of the cost which she enters in her cashflow projection only, including VAT. She also estimates that she will need to draw £1,000 per month to cover her domestic and personal finance requirements, and enters this in her cashflow projection. Her final figure is her Class 2 National Insurance contributions, which she has arranged to pay by standing order out of her business bank account each month. These amount to £5.65 per week (in 1994–95).

Having entered all the figures she thinks are necessary in her profit and cashflow projections, she totals them up so that she can assess the results.

Balance sheet

Unlike a profit and loss account, which gives you information about the trading results of the business over a given period, a balance sheet is a 'snapshot' of what the business owns (*assets*) and what the business owes (*liabilities*) at a single point in time. It will tell you, for example, about the solvency of the business – whether it owns more than it owes or vice versa. The assets of the business include capital equipment, positive bank balance, debtors (what customers owe the business), stocks of goods and so on. Liabilities include overdrawn bank balances, bank loans, trade and other creditors (what the business owes its suppliers, the Inland Revenue, Customs and Excise etc.) and so on.

Ideally, you should produce a projected balance sheet, which will provide you with further information about your business expectations, as well as proving that you have not made any arithmetical errors in your profit and cashflow projections. If you have no accounting knowledge, this can be a tricky exercise and you may need some professional assistance, or alternatively, your local TEC might be able to offer help. However, some banks do not insist that you prepare a balance sheet, depending on the amount and type of finance you are seeking to raise, and you should check this with them in advance.

Judith has managed to prepare a projected balance sheet for her business, with some assistance. It comprises all the assets and liabilities of the business at the end of each month, including the proprietor's current account, which comprises the capital Judith has introduced into the business, her drawings and the profit she has made in the period. The amount of the net assets is the same as the balance on her proprietor's current account – i.e. the balance sheet 'balances'.

If the business were a partnership, the proprietor's current account would be replaced by the partners' current accounts plus the profit or loss for the period. If it were a limited company, it would be replaced by share capital plus, again, the profit or loss for the period.

Judith's projected balance sheet shows her that her assets are greater than her liabilities: the 'Net Assets' figure (at the end of the top half of the balance sheet) is positive at the end of each month. This figure increases each month, which implies that what the business owns is growing faster than what the business owes. If the 'Net Assets' figure were negative (i.e. 'net liabilities') it would warn her that the business owes more than it owns.

Review of the projections

Once you have prepared a first draft of your projections, review them critically. First, are you entirely happy with your estimates? For example:

- Are you sure that you have not over-estimated your sales?
- Have you included *all* your expected costs?
- Have you entered a realistic figure for your own drawings or remuneration each month?
- Have you included all the equipment you need to buy in the first few months?

Work through the profit projection line by line to satisfy yourself that your estimates are as reasonable as possible. Next move on to your cashflow projection and repeat the process. For example:

- Are you sure that customers will pay you as quickly as you have estimated?
- Do you know with certainty that you will be able to open credit accounts with your suppliers, or will they demand cash immediately?

When you are satisfied with each item in your projections, stand back and take a more general view. Do they present the picture of your business that you had expected, or are they much better or worse? Is it as profitable as you expected? Is it generating as much cash as you had envisaged?

If the picture is much better than you had expected, take another careful look at your projections. For example:

- Have you overestimated sales?
- Have you included all categories of expenditure?
- Have you included your own drawings in your cashflow projection?

ABC Office Services
Financial projections for the year ended 30 April 1996
Projected profit and loss account

	May 95	Jun 95	Jul 95	Aug 95	Sep 95	Oct 95	Nov 95	Dec 95	Jan 96	Feb 96	Mar 96	Apr 96	TOTAL
Sales	2,250	2,250	2,750	2,750	3,500	3,500	4,000	4,000	4,000	4,250	4,250	4,250	41,750
Disbursements	100	100	120	120	150	150	175	175	175	190	190	190	1,835
Gross profit	2,150	2,150	2,630	2,630	3,350	3,350	3,825	3,825	3,825	4,060	4,060	4,060	39,915
Motor expenses	150	150	350	150	150	150	175	175	175	175	175	175	2,150
Printing, postage & stationery	75	75	75	75	75	75	100	100	100	100	100	100	1,050
Computer consumables	20	20	20	20	20	20	25	25	25	25	25	25	270
Advertising	25	25	25	25	25	25	25	25	25	25	25	25	300
Salaries	0	0	0	0	0	0	500	500	500	500	500	500	3,000
Employer's National Insurance	0	0	0	0	0	0	28	28	28	28	28	28	168
Insurance	50	50	50	50	50	50	50	50	50	50	50	50	600
Subscriptions	100	0	0	0	0	0	75	0	0	0	0	0	175
Bank charges	8	8	8	8	8	8	8	8	8	8	8	8	96
Repairs and renewals	10	10	10	10	10	10	10	10	10	10	10	10	120
Telephone	75	75	75	75	75	75	75	75	75	75	75	75	900
Training	300	0	0	300	0	0	300	0	0	300	0	0	1,200
Travel	25	25	25	25	25	25	25	25	25	25	25	25	300
Sundry expenses	50	50	50	50	50	50	50	50	50	50	50	50	600
Bank interest payable	16	15	17	12	0	0	0	0	0	0	0	0	60
Depreciation	35	50	69	69	69	89	89	89	89	89	89	89	915
Total overheads	939	553	774	869	557	577	1,535	1,160	1,160	1,460	1,160	1,160	11,904
Net profit for month	1,211	1,597	1,856	1,761	2,793	2,773	2,290	2,665	2,665	2,600	2,900	2,900	28,011

ABC Office Services
Financial projections for the year ended 30 April 1996
Projected cashflow

	May 95	Jun 95	Jul 95	Aug 95	Sep 95	Oct 95	Nov 95	Dec 95	Jan 96	Feb 96	Mar 96	Apr 96	TOTAL
Receipts from sales	0	2,644	2,644	3,231	3,231	4,113	4,113	4,700	4,700	4,700	4,994	4,994	44,064
Capital introduced	2,000	0	0	0	0	0	0	0	0	0	0	0	2,000
Total receipts	2,000	2,644	2,644	3,231	3,231	4,113	4,113	4,700	4,700	4,700	4,994	4,994	46,064
Disbursements	118	118	141	141	176	176	206	206	206	223	223	223	2,157
Motor expenses	176	176	411	176	176	176	206	206	206	206	206	206	2,527
Printing, postage, stationery	88	88	88	88	88	88	118	118	118	118	118	118	1,236
Computer consumables	24	24	24	24	24	24	29	29	29	29	29	29	318
Advertising	29	29	29	29	29	29	29	29	29	29	29	29	348
Salaries – net	0	0	0	0	0	0	427	427	427	427	427	427	2,562
PAYE/National Insurance	0	0	0	0	0	0	0	101	101	101	101	101	505
Insurance	300	0	0	0	0	0	300	0	0	0	0	0	600
Subscriptions	100	0	0	0	0	0	75	0	0	0	0	0	175
Bank charges	8	8	8	8	8	8	8	8	8	8	8	8	96
Repairs and renewals	12	12	12	12	12	12	12	12	12	12	12	12	144
Telephone	0	0	0	264	0	0	264	0	0	264	0	0	792
Training	353	0	0	353	0	0	353	0	0	353	0	0	1,412
Travel	25	25	25	25	25	25	25	25	25	25	25	25	300
Sundry expenses	59	59	59	59	59	59	59	59	59	59	59	59	708
Interest payable	0	16	15	17	12	0	0	0	0	0	0	0	60
Capital equipment	1,974	846	1,072	0	0	1,128	0	0	0	0	0	0	5,020
Value Added Tax	0	0	0	333	0	0	1,200	0	0	1,714	0	0	3,247
Drawings – cash	1,000	1,000	1,000	1,000	1,000	1,000	1,000	1,000	1,000	1,000	1,000	1,000	12,000
Drawings – Class 2 NIC	27	22	27	22	22	27	22	27	27	22	27	22	299
Total payments	4,293	2,423	2,911	2,556	1,631	2,752	4,333	2,247	2,247	4,590	2,264	2,259	34,506
Net cash inflow/(outflow)	(2,293)	221	(267)	675	1,600	1,361	(220)	2,453	2,453	110	2,730	2,735	11,558
Opening bank balance	0	(2,293)	(2,072)	(2,339)	(1,664)	(64)	1,297	1,077	3,530	5,983	6,093	8,823	0
Closing bank balance	(2,293)	(2,072)	(2,339)	(1,664)	(64)	1,297	1,077	3,530	5,983	6,093	8,823	11,558	11,558

ABC Office Services
Financial projections for the year ended 30 April 1996
Projected balance sheet

	May 95	Jun 95	Jul 95	Aug 95	Sep 95	Oct 95	Nov 95	Dec 95	Jan 96	Feb 96	Mar 96	Apr 96
Fixed assets – cost	1,680	2,400	3,312	3,312	3,312	4,272	4,272	4,272	4,272	4,272	4,272	4,272
Fixed assets – depreciation	35	85	154	223	292	381	470	559	648	737	826	915
	1,645	2,315	3,158	3,089	3,020	3,891	3,802	3,713	3,624	3,535	3,446	3,357
Current Assets												
Debtors	2,644	2,644	3,231	3,232	4,113	4,113	4,700	4,700	4,700	4,994	4,994	4,994
Bank account	(2,293)	(2,072)	(2,339)	(1,664)	(64)	1,297	1,077	3,530	5,983	6,093	8,823	11,558
Other debtors	250	200	150	100	50	0	250	200	150	100	50	0
	601	772	1,042	1,668	4,099	5,410	6,027	8,430	10,833	11,187	13,867	16,552
Current liabilities												
Creditors	103	190	279	98	174	262	85	172	259	82	170	258
PAYE/NIC	0	0	0	0	0	0	101	101	101	101	101	101
VAT	(41)	138	333	337	852	1,200	536	1,125	1,174	578	1,208	1,838
	62	328	612	435	1,026	1,462	722	1,398	2,074	761	1,479	2,197
Net Current Assets	539	444	430	1,233	3,073	3,948	5,305	7,032	8,759	10,426	12,388	14,355
Net Assets	2,184	2,759	3,588	4,322	6,093	7,839	9,107	10,745	12,383	13,961	15,834	17,712
Proprietor's current account												
Capital introduced	2,000	2,000	2,000	2,000	2,000	2,000	2,000	2,000	2,000	2,000	2,000	2,000
Drawings	(1,027)	(2,049)	(3,076)	(4,103)	(5,125)	(6,152)	(7,174)	(8,201)	(9,228)	(10,250)	(11,277)	(12,299)
Profit for period	1,211	2,808	4,664	6,425	9,218	11,991	14,281	16,946	19,611	22,211	25,111	28,011
	2,184	2,759	3,588	4,322	6,093	7,839	9,107	10,745	12,383	13,961	15,834	17,712

If the projections present a worse picture than you were expecting, look for areas where improvements could be achieved. For example:

- Have you pitched your sales prices too low?
- Can you cut back your overheads?
- Can you reduce the amount of cash which you draw out of the business for personal and domestic purposes?

Do be aware also that you will have to pay tax on any profits generated by your business, and you will need to ensure that sufficient cash is available in the bank account to cover your tax liabilities when they arise.

When you are satisfied with your projections, consider the implications of unexpected improvements or deteriorations in your figures. Select the variables which are most critical to your business, and calculate the effect on your profit and cashflow if circumstances change unexpectedly. For example, the level of sales generated by ABC Office Services and prompt receipt of cash is vital to the business. In the second set of projections prepared by Judith, she calculates the effect of a 20 per cent drop in sales each month, combined with a delay of an extra 30 days before she receives payment. She has assumed that her overheads will remain the same at the reduced level of sales.

Her projected profit and loss account shows that her profit before tax for the year is reduced from £28,011 to £19,379, a drop of some 30 per cent. Perhaps more critically, the cashflow projection shows that her bank balance is overdrawn throughout the whole year, whereas previously she had required an overdraft only until month six, after which the bank balance increased steadily. While she believes that this picture of her business is unnecessarily pessimistic, she feels that she will be better prepared to cope with unexpected problems if she has some idea beforehand of the impact they will have on her business.

Depending on the nature of your business, you might examine the effect of altering different variables, such as sales, cost of sales, cash receipts, payments to suppliers for goods and so on.

Using your projections

Most people tend to prepare projections for their business only when it is required by their bank, local TEC and so on. However, they should be of most use to *you*, the business owner. You have taken the time to research and prepare them, so make sure that you use them once the business is underway. You might use them as a basis for setting targets, or as a means of measuring actual business performance to assess whether it matches up to expectations.

ABC Office Services
Financial projections for the year ended 30 April 1996
Projected profit and loss account (revised)

	May 95	Jun 95	Jul 95	Aug 95	Sep 95	Oct 95	Nov 95	Dec 95	Jan 96	Feb 96	Mar 96	Apr 96	TOTAL
Sales	1,800	1,800	2,200	2,200	2,800	2,800	3,200	3,200	3,200	3,400	3,400	3,400	33,400
Disbursements	100	100	120	120	150	150	175	175	175	190	190	190	1,835
Gross profit	1,700	1,700	2,080	2,080	2,650	2,650	3,025	3,025	3,025	3,210	3,210	3,210	31,565
Motor expenses	150	150	350	150	150	150	175	175	175	175	175	175	2,150
Printing, postage, stationery	75	75	75	75	75	75	100	100	100	100	100	100	1,050
Computer consumables	20	20	20	20	20	20	25	25	25	25	25	25	270
Advertising	25	25	25	25	25	25	25	25	25	25	25	25	300
Salaries	0	0	0	0	0	0	500	500	500	500	500	500	3,000
Employer's National Insurance	0	0	0	0	0	0	28	28	28	28	28	28	168
Insurance	50	50	50	50	50	50	50	50	50	50	50	50	600
Subscriptions	100	0	0	0	0	0	75	0	50	0	0	0	175
Bank charges	8	8	8	8	8	8	8	8	8	8	8	8	96
Repairs and renewals	10	10	10	10	10	10	10	10	10	10	10	10	120
Telephone	75	75	75	75	75	75	75	75	75	75	75	75	900
Training	300	0	0	300	0	0	300	0	0	300	0	0	1,200
Travel	25	25	25	25	25	25	25	25	25	25	25	25	300
Sundry expenses	50	50	50	50	50	50	50	50	50	50	50	50	600
Bank interest payable	16	33	39	41	34	36	41	34	23	26	16	4	342
Depreciation	35	50	69	69	69	89	89	89	89	89	89	89	915
Total overheads	939	571	796	898	591	613	1,576	1,194	1,183	1,486	1,176	1,164	12,186
Net profit for month	761	1,129	1,284	1,182	2,059	2,037	1,449	1,831	1,842	1,724	2,034	2,046	19,379

ABC Office Services
Financial projections for the year ended 30 April 1996
Projected cashflow (revised)

	May 95	Jun 95	Jul 95	Aug 95	Sep 95	Oct 95	Nov 95	Dec 95	Jan 96	Feb 96	Mar 96	Apr 96	TOTAL
Receipts from sales	0	0	2,115	2,115	2,585	2,585	3,290	3,290	3,760	3,760	3,760	3,995	31,256
Capital introduced	2,000	0										0	2,000
Total receipts	2,000	0	2,115	2,115	2,585	2,585	3,290	3,290	3,760	3,760	3,760	3,995	33,256
Disbursements	118	118	141	141	176	176	206	206	206	223	223	223	2,157
Motor expenses	176	176	411	176	176	176	206	206	206	206	206	206	2,527
Printing, postage, stationery	88	88	88	88	88	88	118	118	118	118	118	118	1,236
Computer consumables	24	24	24	24	24	24	29	29	29	29	29	29	318
Advertising	29	29	29	29	29	29	29	29	29	29	29	29	348
Salaries – net	0	0	0	0	0	0	427	427	427	427	427	427	2,562
PAYE/National Insurance	0	0	0	0	0	0	0	101	101	101	101	101	505
Insurance	300	0	0	0	0	0	300	0	0	0	0	0	600
Subscriptions	100	0	0	0	0	0	75	0	0	0	0	0	175
Bank charges	8	8	8	8	8	8	8	8	8	8	8	8	96
Repairs and renewals	12	12	12	12	12	12	12	12	12	12	12	12	144
Telephone	0	0	0	264	0	0	264	0	0	264	0	0	792
Training	353	0	0	353	0	0	353	0	0	353	0	0	1,412
Travel	25	25	25	25	25	25	25	25	25	25	25	25	300
Sundry expenses	59	59	59	59	59	59	59	59	59	59	59	59	708
Interest payable	0	16	33	39	41	34	36	41	34	23	26	16	339
Capital equipment	1,974	846	1,072	0	0	1,128	0	0	0	0	0	0	5,020
Value Added Tax	0	0	0	79	0	0	858	0	0	1,294	0	0	2,232
Drawings – cash	1,000	1,000	1,000	1,000	1,000	1,000	1,000	1,000	1,000	1,000	1,000	1,000	12,000
Drawings – Class 2 NIC	27	22	27	27	22	27	22	27	27	22	27	22	299
Total payments	4,293	2,423	2,930	2,325	1,660	2,786	4,027	2,288	2,281	4,193	2,290	2,274	33,770
Net cash inflow/(outflow)	(2,293)	(2,422)	(815)	(210)	925	(200)	(737)	1,002	1,479	(433)	1,470	1,721	(513)
Opening bank balance	0	(2,293)	(4,716)	(5,530)	(5,740)	(4,816)	(5,016)	(5,753)	(4,750)	(3,271)	(3,704)	(2,234)	0
Closing bank balance	(2,293)	(4,716)	(5,530)	(5,740)	(4,816)	(5,016)	(5,753)	(4,750)	(3,271)	(3,704)	(2,234)	(513)	(513)

ABC Office Services
Financial projections for the year ended 30 April 1996.
Projected balance sheet (revised)

	May 95	Jun 95	Jul 95	Aug 95	Sep 95	Oct 95	Nov 95	Dec 95	Jan 96	Feb 96	Mar 96	Apr 96
Fixed assets – cost	1,680	2,400	3,312	3,312	3,312	4,272	4,272	4,272	4,272	4,272	4,272	4,272
Fixed assets – depreciation	35	85	154	223	292	381	470	559	648	737	826	915
	1,645	2,315	3,158	3,089	3,020	3,891	3,802	3,713	3,624	3,535	3,446	3,357
Current Assets												
Debtors	2,115	4,230	4,700	5,170	5,875	6,580	7,050	7,520	7,520	7,755	7,990	7,990
Bank account	(2,293)	(4,716)	(5,530)	(5,740)	(4,816)	(5,016)	(5,753)	(4,750)	(3,271)	(3,704)	(2,234)	(513)
Other debtors	250	200	150	100	50	0	250	200	150	100	50	0
	72	(285)	(680)	(470)	1,110	1,565	1,547	2,970	4,399	4,151	5,806	7,477
Current liabilities												
Creditors	103	209	302	127	207	298	126	206	283	108	186	262
PAYE/NIC	0	0	0	0	0	0	101	101	101	101	101	101
VAT	(120)	(19)	79	241	634	858	396	845	1,294	429	910	1,391
	(17)	189	381	367	841	1,156	622	1,151	1,677	638	1,197	1,754
Net Current Assets	89	(475)	(1,062)	(837)	269	409	925	1,818	2,722	3,513	4,609	5,723
Net Assets	1,734	1,840	2,096	2,251	3,289	4,300	4,727	5,531	6,346	7,048	8,055	9,080
Proprietor's current account												
Capital introduced	2,000	2,000	2,000	2,000	2,000	2,000	2,000	2,000	2,000	2,000	2,000	2,000
Drawings	(1,027)	(2,049)	(3,076)	(4,103)	(5,125)	(6,152)	(7,174)	(8,201)	(9,228)	(10,250)	(11,277)	(12,299)
Profit for period	761	1,889	3,172	4,355	6,414	8,452	9,901	11,732	13,574	15,298	17,332	19,379
	1,734	1,840	2,096	2,252	3,289	4,300	4,727	5,531	6,346	7,048	8,055	9,080

You may find later that the results for your business bear little resemblance to the figures you put in your projections. They may be much better or worse; in either case it is useful to look back at your projections and try to work out why your estimates were not more accurate. If you simply underestimated the success of your business, then congratulate yourself – then think ahead about how you will maintain that success. If your business has performed much worse than you had hoped, are there any lessons that you can learn? It may be useful to discuss with your accountant the differences between your projections and your year-end accounts, and how any particular weaknesses might be resolved in the future.

A small printing business gained some valuable information from this exercise at the end of their first year of trading. The two partners had prepared financial projections in which they had set their selling prices as low as possible while still making a small profit, on the basis that this was the best means of gaining customers. When they examined their actual trading results, they discovered that their selling prices had been too low to allow for the price increases they had suffered from their suppliers, and the business had made a fairly substantial loss in the first year. Although they had been aware during the year that their bank overdraft was much larger than they had anticipated from their projections, they had not realized the extent to which the price increase had affected their trading performance. They resolved in future to pay far more attention to the effect of changes in suppliers' prices on their profitability, which paid off in the form of much improved results in the following two years.

Preparing a business plan

If you intend to approach outside sources to raise finance for your business, you may need to prepare a full business plan. Beside your financial projections, a business plan sets out details of your business activity, how it will operate, who will run it, who you will sell to, your plans for its future, and so on. If you have never been involved in the preparation of a business plan before, the task may seem a daunting one. It will take time, it will need careful thought and research, and you may need to draw on external help. But once the document has been prepared, it can be used as a basis for future assessment of business performance when the business is underway. Furthermore, it is a useful exercise for focusing on how you see the development of the business in its infancy.

The main elements of a business plan are:

- concluding summary – what is the product or service, what is the market and what are its prospects of success, how much finance is needed and why;

- a description of the proposed business activity and the business itself;
- a description of the market you are operating in, where you fit into it and how you propose to sell your product or service;
- your business aims, both for the short and the longer term, and how you plan to achieve them;
- the person or people running the business, including a curriculum vitae, a description of their particular skills and how these will benefit the business. This is a very important section – remember that you are selling yourself and your skills as well as the business idea to potential lenders;
- a summary of projected results and the finance required, based on the projections you have prepared (as described in 'Financial Projections' above);
- an appendix setting out your detailed financial projections and underlying assumptions;
- any other relevant appendices which are too long or technical to be included in the main body of the text, such as detailed product specifications.

It may seem odd to put the concluding summary at the beginning of the plan, but this will communicate to the reader at the very outset the essence of your plan and the main salient facts.

Your plan does not need to be long. Indeed, an unnecessarily long business plan which includes too much technical detail or flowery description is unlikely to hold the interest of the reader. If you feel it is essential to include, for example, long and detailed technical descriptions, put these in an appendix at the end of the plan. Keep the text concise and to the point: bank managers and financiers read a large number of business plans and are skilled at detecting those which contain only woolly ideas shrouded in pages of rambling narrative.

The appearance of your business plan is also of crucial importance. Here are some guidelines for presentation:

- type the text and bind and/or secure it in some way that prevents pages slipping out and going astray;
- set out the text so that it does not cause the reader to lose interest after the first sentence;
- avoid very long paragraphs – make sure there are plenty of breaks in the text;
- use headings and subheadings sensibly;
- consider numbering sections and subsections of the plan for maximum clarity. For example, the first section might be numbered as follows:

1	Concluding summary
1.1	The product
1.2	The market
1.3	Prospects
1.4	Finance required

- create an index and set it out as shown by the numbered sections above, so that the reader can refer to particular parts of the plan easily.

Preparing a business plan is a valuable exercise for anyone who intends to set up their own business. Even if you prepare only a short document, it will help to clarify in your own mind exactly how you intend your business to work, what you are trying to achieve and how you expect to do that. Your ideas will become more concrete and better defined, which will benefit the business in its early stages. Additionally, if you need in the future to prepare a business plan in order to raise finance, or a résumé of the business to present to potential new customers, you already have a skeleton plan which you can build on or amend to suit the circumstances.

Sources and types of finance

If you have prepared profit and cashflow projections for your business, you should have a reasonable idea of the level of finance you will need to cover your start-up costs and to provide sufficient working capital throughout the first year of trading. It is worth stressing again that although projections are necessarily only estimates, there is no other means of gaining any reasonable idea of the amount of finance you will need. You will then have to decide on the most appropriate type of finance for your business, which will vary according to the nature of your business and the level of finance you are seeking. Some of the most popular sources of funds include:

- banks – overdraft or loan
- venture capital
- own savings/family/redundancy settlement.

Banks

For many people, the bank is the first option they consider when trying to raise finance. If you have a good credit record and know your bank manager reasonably well, you may feel that this is your best chance of securing the financial support you need. However, it may not be your own bank manager who takes the decision whether or not to lend to you. In small branches, the decision might well be referred to a regional head office

— so do not dismiss the other options available. If you are seeking finance to cover your start-up costs, banks may also want some evidence that you are putting some of your own money into the business. After all, if you are not prepared to invest in your own venture, why should they?

Bank overdraft

The advantage of a bank overdraft is that, up to your agreed overdraft limit, you borrow only the amount you need at any given time and pay interest only on that amount. There will be a charge for setting up the facility, and a periodic renewal fee if you continue to need the overdraft after, say, a year. The bank will probably demand some form of security, such as a charge over your business assets or your home, or a personal guarantee. The disadvantage of an overdraft is that the bank is entitled to call for immediate repayment at any time, and although this is unlikely if you operate within your overdraft limit, it can happen. If you are unable to repay the money and have given a personal guarantee, this could spell financial ruin for your business and for you personally. In the most severe circumstances, you might be forced to wind up your business and sell your home in order to satisfy your debts. It is often the most suitable form of finance if you require only a small amount of money, to get the business off the ground or to cover short-term working capital deficits in the early months. However, the bank will expect the overdraft to reduce or at least fluctuate during the period: if your bank balance is constantly at or around a substantial overdraft limit, the bank might seek to convert it to a longer-term loan.

In the case of ABC Office Services, the original set of projections show a maximum overdrawn bank balance during the year of just over £2,300, but the balance increases in the more pessimistic projections to over £5,700 in months four and seven. Judith decides to err on the side of caution and to seek an overdraft facility of £6,000 for the first twelve months. She decides that this is the most appropriate form of borrowing for her, since she is unsure whether she will need to use the full facility, and it will give her maximum flexibility.

Bank loan

A bank loan tends to be more appropriate when you need to borrow a larger sum of money over a longer period, to finance a major purchase of machinery for example. Again there will be a fee for arranging the loan, and the interest charge may either be a fixed percentage or at a pre-arranged percentage over the bank's base rate, so that the interest rate fluctuates with the base rate. The repayments will be negotiated in advance to pay off the loan over the agreed period, which might range from a few years to up to 25 or 30 years. As with an overdraft, security or a personal guarantee will be required.

Venture capital

Traditionally, smaller businesses have been put off using venture capital as a source of finance. It is often assumed that venture capitalists are looking to invest very substantial sums and that smaller businesses simply do not represent a suitable proposition. This is not necessarily true, although they are interested primarily in businesses which are profitable and fast growing, and that will develop significantly over the next few years. You will also need to demonstrate the high quality of the people involved in running the business, that they have strong commercial and managerial skills and use them to their full advantage for the business. Alternatively, you may be able to find an individual investor with sound business experience who is willing to invest not only money but also time in your business.

Investment of this type does mean that a degree of control over the business will have to be relinquished to your investor, and for this reason alone many people do not consider venture capital as a suitable option for their business.

The Department of Trade and Industry (DTI) produce a booklet *Finance without debt – A guide to sources of venture capital under £250,000*, which contains some useful advice and guidelines to judge whether venture capital is an option worth considering for your business. Additionally, Stoy Hayward (telephone 0171 486 5888) produce an annual *Venture Capital Guide*, which contains a list of some of the sources of venture capital and descriptions of the types of investment that corporate investors are seeking to make. The British Venture Capital Association (telephone 0171 240 3846) also publishes a directory of their members, including the levels of investment they will consider, the industry sectors and geographical areas in which they are particularly interested, and so on.

The British Venture Capital Association also produces *A Directory of Business Introduction Services*, which sets out details of a number of organizations which aim to match individual investors, known as 'business angels', with businesses seeking investment. Business angels will typically invest between £10,000 and £50,000 at a time, for at least three to five years, and possibly longer. They will obviously be seeking a return on their investment, and will at some stage require an 'exit' for their investment. Many business angels are keen to participate in the running of the business in which they invest, and you may be able to benefit from either specialist skills, such as finance or marketing, or general business management skills.

If you are looking for an individual rather than a corporate investor, one organization worth approaching is the Local Investment Networking Company (telephone 0171 236 3000). LINC is run by a number of independent, privately owned agencies located throughout the UK. It works as an introduction service between investors and businesses seeking start-up and growth capital, and sends out bulletins to potential investors listing businesses which are seeking finance. There is no guarantee of success, and your business or business idea would be subject to some investigation to ensure that it is suitable for inclusion in their bulletin.

Own finance

You may prefer not to turn to outside sources of finance at all, but to provide the funds yourself to get the business started. If the level of finance you require is not that great, and you have sufficient savings or a redundancy settlement to meet your needs, this may be a feasible option.

Other members of your family may also be prepared to help. However, ensure that all parties are absolutely clear about the risks they might be taking by putting money into your new venture. It may be some time before you are in a position to repay their loan or investment, and they must realize that you will not be able simply to write them a cheque if they decide they are suddenly in need of funds themselves. The potential distress caused in this type of situation can be a major disadvantage, although you may find that presenting your case for finance to family members is more successful and easier than approaching external lenders or investors.

Conclusions

Do not try to guess at the level of finance you will require to get your business started. If you prepare even simple financial projections, you will be in a far stronger position to make a realistic assessment. You may not need to prepare a full business plan if you are not approaching external sources of finance, but it can be a helpful exercise to focus on all the elements of the plan and to determine how your business will work in practice. It is far easier to spend time planning and researching now than to discover later that the business will not work.

4 Accounting records and administration

In the early stages of setting up and running a new business you will have to maintain your accounting records and the associated paperwork, deal with your general administration and decide whether or not a computer will help you run your business more effectively. These things may not seem a priority. You will probably feel excited and perhaps rather nervous at the prospect of being in business on your own. Will you succeed in winning enough customers or clients? Have you planned your finances adequately to provide sufficient funds for the business and for you personally? These issues are likely to occupy your thoughts to a far greater extent than the more mundane and apparently less productive business of taking care of your paperwork. Dealing with customers, bankers, suppliers and so on is of critical importance, but so too is keeping on top of the surprisingly large quantities of paper which will be generated.

If you are completely new to running your own business, the process of dealing with accounting records and administration may at first be a daunting prospect, simply because of its unfamiliarity. But do not delay action. General administrative tasks – whether ensuring that your time records are up-to-date, returning telephone messages, going through the morning's mail or sending out invoices to customers – are important right from the outset, even if they sometimes seem unnecessarily time-consuming. Few people actually enjoy these tasks, but after a short time, most come to realize that they are an integral part of any business and best dealt with as swiftly as possible.

It will take time to develop a routine, but the important point is that you do not ignore these tasks. They form a part of the overall management of your business and need to be controlled. Depending on the type of business you are running, you may find later that it is more efficient and cost-effective to employ somebody else, perhaps on a part-time or *ad hoc* basis at first, to provide you with bookkeeping and administrative support. Alternatively, perhaps your spouse or partner is in a position to offer some help.

The rest of this chapter looks in some detail at how you might organize your accounting records and the associated administration, at whether the use of a computer might help to streamline some of your paperwork, and at the importance of effective time management.

The emphasis on bookkeeping and accounting reflects their importance in providing you with vital information. Imagine that you receive no bank statements for a year for your personal bank account; you keep no records of your cheque payments and have no idea what your bank balance is. The only information you receive is letters from your bank manager saying that you have exceeded your overdraft limit again. How do you check your income? How do you plan your expenditure? In short, you can't. The same applies to keeping accounting records for your business. It has been said: 'If you can't control the accounts – the very heartbeat of a company – you're in trouble.'

Bookkeeping and accounting systems

Accurate accounting records help you to keep track of how your business is performing and to make accurate and informed decisions. Your records will tell you who owes the business money, to whom the business owes money, what the bank account balance is, and so on. You may feel that you can store this information in your head at first, but as your volume of transactions increases you will find it much easier if an effective system is in place for recording these details.

Additionally, accounts will have to be prepared whether your business is a sole trade, a partnership or a limited company. These will be submitted to the Inland Revenue as they will form the basis of your income tax or corporation tax liabilities. While the accounts and tax computations themselves are likely to be prepared by your accountant, it will be made considerably more straightforward – and cheaper – if he or she is able to work from good accounting records.

If you are registered for Value Added Tax, you will also need details of your output (sales) and input (purchases) VAT and net sales and purchases for your quarterly or monthly VAT returns. These can all be extracted from properly maintained accounting records. Additionally, if you are trading within a limited company, the Companies Act requires the directors to take responsibility for ensuring that adequate books and records are maintained.

The most important point to realize is that you can benefit from a bookkeeping and accounting system from the very outset of the business. It does not need to be sophisticated or complicated, provided that it is accurate, logical and appropriate for your business. You will also avoid the need to spend valuable time wading through backlogs of paperwork later on if it is set up immediately.

Computerized accounting system

You may prefer to use computer software to maintain your accounts. This can be a better option if you have a lot of transactions and you find data input at a keyboard more efficient than manual recording. A vast range of accounting software is available, from fairly straightforward bookkeeping packages suitable for relatively novice bookkeepers, to more sophisticated packages which demand a detailed knowledge of accounting principles for really effective use.

The majority of packages demand both computer literacy and some accounting knowledge, or at least sufficient understanding of accounting principles to ensure that the information and reports produced by the software make sense. Do beware of purchasing and implementing advanced-level accounting software with only a hazy understanding of how it should be used: the resulting confusion may be expensive and time-consuming to correct.

A further consideration is the cost of implementing the system. If you already own or are intending to purchase a computer and printer for other purposes, the additional costs will be only for the software and training – either from an accountant or a specialist software trainer. If not, the costs could mount up, although it may still be worthwhile for the business to choose this option. As well as the financial cost, do not underestimate the time you will need to spend becoming familiar with the software and ensuring you understand properly how to enter transactions, produce reports and so on.

A family-owned hotel business wanted to purchase software which would track room occupancy and the use by guests of other facilities such as the bar and restaurant, and which would also link with an accounting function. The very sensible rationale behind the decision was that the billing of guests and the maintenance of accounting records could be combined, avoiding the need to run two separate systems. It was also important that sales could be analysed between rooms, food and drinks and other miscellaneous items such as telephone, laundry and so on. The proprietor purchased a system which seemed ideal. It only emerged later that although the hotel billing module of the software operated correctly, it did not link correctly with the accounting functions, largely because it had not originally been designed to do so. Fortunately, the problem was identified by the proprietor quickly, so that it was remedied before too much confusion was caused. However, he now recommends anybody purchasing specialist software to make absolutely sure, by means of several detailed demonstrations if necessary, that it is both able to meet the specific requirements of your business and that the software itself does not have any weak links.

Basic manual bookkeeping system

If computerized accounting records do not seem appropriate for your business, a basic manual bookkeeping system is cheap and straightforward to set up. If properly maintained, it will provide you with sufficient information to keep track of the business's financial position.

While no business has 'standard' bookkeeping requirements, you will need books which record:

- sales;
- purchases;
- bank account payments and receipts;
- cash expenses;
- wages and salaries (if applicable).

The examples given below are neither definitive nor exhaustive, but set out basic guidelines for a simple manual bookkeeping system. It is assumed in these examples that the business is registered for VAT.

Sales

If you are running the type of business in which you need to send out sales invoices to your customers, try to make sure that you do so as quickly as possible. Remember that the sooner you send out the invoice, the sooner you can expect payment. Try not to leave this task, say, to the end of the month: if your customers automatically pay on a 30- or 60-day cycle, you could wait several weeks more than necessary for your money.

Your invoices should contain the following details:

- business name and address;
- VAT registration number (if applicable);
- company registration number, if a limited company;
- unique sequential invoice number;
- customer name and address;
- tax point, i.e the date at which the supply is made;
- details of goods or service, including the rate of VAT charged;
- net value excluding VAT;
- any discount allowed;
- VAT;
- gross value including VAT.

You should always keep a copy of the invoice for the business's own records.

Note that if you make sales to countries within the European Union other than the UK, the *customer's* VAT registration number must also appear on the sales invoice. Even though the rate of VAT charged will be zero, this must be included on the invoice.

You will quickly realize that managing your business is made much easier if you have an effective system for filing all your invoices and other paperwork. When you have prepared and sent out your sales invoices, file them sequentially in a file marked 'Unpaid Sales Invoices'. When you receive payment for an invoice, transfer it to a separate file marked 'Paid Sales Invoices', and note on the invoice the date payment is received. You now have the beginnings of a system which tells who has paid you and who owes you money.

You should also keep a 'Sales Day Book' to record summarized details of all your sales invoices and the date payment is received. You will find this gives you vital information about the level of sales you are making, as well a allowing you to see at a glance which customers owe the business money at any time. You should enter details in the Sales Day Book from your copy sales invoices, and you might set it out as follows:

Invoice date	Customer	Invoice number	Gross	VAT	Net	Date paid
10.1.95	Henderson	1001	998.75	148.75	850.00	31.1.95
17.1.95	Cornwall	1002	881.25	131.25	750.00	
22.1.95	Taylor	1003	822.50	122.50	700.00	23.1.95
25.1.95	Neal	1004	940.00	140.00	800.00	
31.1.95	Walden	1005	740.25	110.25	630.00	31.1.95
JANUARY TOTAL			4,382.75	652.75	3,730.00	

If you make different types of sales, it may be useful to have several 'Net' columns, into which these different categories can be analysed, so that you can monitor sales performance more easily. Similarly, if you make sales to countries in the European Union other than UK, these might be analysed into a separate column since you will need to declare this information separately on your VAT returns.

At the end of each month, total all of the columns. Check that the total of the 'Net' plus the 'VAT' columns is the same as the total of the 'Gross' column. If it is not, you have made a mistake, which you should find and correct before proceeding any further.

In the example above, it is now easy to see that invoices 1001, 1003 and 1005 have already been paid, but 1002 and 1004 are still outstanding. Depending on your credit terms, you might want to contact these customers now to chase up their payment.

You can also see immediately the level of sales you have made in the month. The 'Gross' column tells you how much cash you can expect to receive in respect of those sales, while the 'Net' column is the figure you are interested in from the point of view of trading performance. Monitoring your sales is now very straightforward and will help you to make decisions about whether you are generating sufficient business.

As well as all this information, the VAT column of your book provides you with the net sales and 'Output VAT' (sales VAT) details you need for your VAT return, which will save you time and effort later.

Purchases

Your purchases are the goods and services you buy to maintain your business. They might range from goods which you buy for resale to advertising, telephone, training costs and so on.

You will want to keep a careful check on your purchases and overheads, especially in the early stages, to make sure they are kept at a level which is appropriate for your business. As with your sales, the best way to do this is to make sure that all invoices are filed logically and their details are recorded. You will then be able to keep track of how you are spending your money.

You should keep invoices for all the goods and services purchased by the business. At this stage of your bookkeeping, you are concerned only with items which you will pay for through your business bank account. It is a good idea to mark all invoices with your own unique sequential number (e.g. P1, P2 etc.) for reference purposes and file them in an 'Unpaid purchase invoices' file in numerical order until they are paid. When you pay them, note the cheque number (or other reference, such as 'Paid by direct debit') and date on the invoice before transferring them to a 'Paid purchase invoices' file, again in numerical order.

To make it easier to monitor your expenditure on different categories of cost, you will enter your purchase invoice details in a 'Purchase Day Book'. This will be of most use to you if the net value of each purchase invoice is analysed into separate columns of the book which represent different types of expense. This analysis will have to be performed at some stage for the preparation of your year-end accounts, so you can save time and costs by doing it yourself. More importantly for you at this stage, it will allow you to monitor the level of expenditure by the business on different types of expenses.

You might set out your Purchase Day Book as follows:

Invoice date	Supplier	Invoice number	Gross	VAT	Goods for resale	Printing and Stat'ery	Light and Heat	Prof. fees	Date Paid/ Cheque
5.1.95	Walter	P1	411.25	61.25	350.00				26.1.95 000005
9.1.95	Bellprint	P2	235.00	35.00		200.00			9.1.95 000001
13.1.95	Walter	P3	881.25	131.25	750.00				31.1.95 000008
17.1.95	East Electric	P4	160.98	23.98			137.00		28.1.95 000007
23.1.95	Oakstead & Co.	P5	293.75	43.75				250.00	
28.1.95	Walter	P6	998.75	148.75	850.00				
JANUARY TOTAL			2,980.98	443.98	1,950.00	200.00	137.00	250.00	

What does your Purchase Day Book tell you? First it is easy to see who you have paid already, and which suppliers are still owed money. In the example above, invoices P1 to P4 have already been paid, but P5 and P6 are still outstanding. Depending on the credit terms of your suppliers, this might act as a prompt to you that you should now send them a cheque.

It also gives you an instant analysis of your purchase invoices. If expenditure on any category looks unusually high or low, this will be immediately obvious. For example, if you normally expect invoices totalling around £150 a month for advertising, and this month the total is £350, you are quickly alerted to the fact. Perhaps an error has been made in the invoice, or perhaps there has been a dramatic price increase. Whatever the reason, you have the information at your fingertips, and can investigate and take any necessary action straight away.

As with your Sales Day Book, the VAT column of your Purchase Day Book will also provide some of the details you need for your VAT return, which will avoid the need to go through your invoices again to work out the 'input VAT' (purchases VAT) you can reclaim.

Bank account

One of the figures that will probably concern you most is the balance on your business bank account. You will want to make sure that you don't suffer heavy bank charges or interest from an unauthorized overdraft, or if you have an agreed overdraft, that you don't exceed its limit. If you do not have your own records of bank payments and receipts (other than cheque books and paying-in books), then your only means of checking your bank balance will be to wait until you receive your bank statement at the end of the month. It is very easy, especially if you make certain payments by direct debit or standing order, to lose track of your bank balance, however carefully you think you are monitoring it.

To make sure that you keep control over your bank account, and to help you judge when or whether you can pay large amounts to suppliers or need to chase customers urgently for payment, you will need a record of all the transactions which pass through the business bank account. Confusingly, this is known as the 'Cash Book' (although it has nothing to do with 'cash' *per se*) and it should mirror all the details and amounts shown on the business's bank statements. This will help you to manage your cashflow, rather than allowing your bank balance to come as a shock at the end of the month.

The Cash Book is split into two sections, one for receipts and the other for payments.

BANK RECEIPTS

When you pay amounts into the business bank account, write down full details of these amounts on the paying-in slip: for example, 'Personal Capital Introduced £2,000' or 'Henderson invoice 1001 £998.75'. If you omit these details, it can be difficult to remember them later when you are entering the details in your Cash Book.

All amounts paid into the business bank account, both from customers and other sources (bank interest, refunds of VAT etc.) are recorded in the 'receipts' section of the Cash Book, from the details which you wrote in your paying-in book.

The example below shows that the proprietor has paid in some personal cash, his Enterprise Allowance for the week, and receipts from three customers who have paid their sales invoices. Although there is a 'VAT' column in the Cash Book, you will enter bank receipts from customers in respect of sales invoices recorded in your Sales Day Book without analysing the VAT separately. You have already analysed the VAT in the Sales Day Book, and it is not necessary to analyse the VAT again (unless you have opted to account for VAT on the 'Cash Accounting Basis' – talk to your accountant if this is the case). You therefore enter the gross amounts received from customers including VAT both in the 'Gross' column and in the 'Sales Day Book' column, as shown below. The sales invoice number is entered in the 'Ref' column, to provide a means of cross-reference to the Sales Day Book.

At the same time, go back to your Sales Day Book and write the date payment is received from the customer in the 'Date paid' column against the invoice in question. You will then be able to keep track of exactly who has paid you and who still owes you money.

Date	Description	Ref	Gross	VAT	Sales Day Book	Other
7.1.95	Cash introduced	–	2,000.00			2,000.00
15.1.95	Enterprise Allowance	–	40.00			40.00
23.1.95	Taylor	1003	822.50		822.50	
31.1.95	Henderson	1001	998.75		998.75	
31.1.95	Walden	1005	740.25		740.25	
JANUARY TOTAL			4,601.50		2,561.50	2,040.00

At the end of each month, add up each of the columns. The sum of the 'Gross' column should be the same as the total of all other columns. If it is not, you should find the mistake and correct it before continuing.

It is a good idea to wait until you have received your monthly bank statement before adding up the columns, so that you can check that there are no items on the statement which you have missed out, such as bank interest received.

You should now have a complete record of all the amounts paid into your business bank account.

BANK PAYMENTS

Bank payments are recorded in the 'payments' section of the Cash Book. You should enter details from cheque stubs in cheque number order, and where necessary wait for your monthly bank statement for details of direct debits, standing orders and other similar payments.

In the example below, the proprietor has paid purchase invoice numbers P1 to P4, paid for some petrol by business cheque, drawn out some cash for himself and entered details of bank charges and interest from his bank statement.

You will see that for payments to suppliers whose invoices are recorded in the Purchase Day Book, you do not need to enter the VAT again in the Cash Book when the invoice is paid (again, unless you have opted to account for VAT on the 'Cash accounting basis', in which case discuss this with your accountant). You have already analysed the VAT in the Purchase Day Book. Simply enter the gross amount including VAT in both the 'Gross' and the 'Purchase Day Book' columns.

At the same time, enter the date paid and the cheque number in the Purchase Day Book against the relevant invoice, as shown in the example above. You will now be able to see exactly who you have paid and which suppliers are still owed money. As with the Purchase Day Book, the headings you need will vary from business to business, depending on the types of payment you encounter most frequently.

Date	Payee	Ref	Cheque number	Gross	VAT	Purchase Day Book	Cash	Bank Chg/Int	Rent	Petrol
9.1.95	Bellprint	P2	000001	235.00		235.00				
10.1.95	Cash – self		000002	200.00			200.00			
14.1.95	Jarrold		000003	750.00					750.00	
20.1.95	Cash – self		000004	150.00			150.00			
26.1.95	Walter	P1	000005	411.25		411.25				
27.1.95	Cash – self		000006	150.00			150.00			
28.1.95	East Elect	P4	000007	160.98		160.98				
31.1.95	Walter	P3	000008	881.25		881.25				
31.1.95	Beech S/stn		000009	25.00	3.72					21.28
26.1.95	Bank charges	—		20.00				20.00		
26.1.95	Bank interest	—		11.26				11.26		
JANUARY TOTAL				2,994.74	3.72	1,688.48	500.00	31.26	750.00	21.28

When you receive your business bank statement for the month, check it to make sure that you have not missed any transactions out of the Cash Book. It is easy to forget to enter bank charges and interest or direct debit payments. Remember that the purpose of the Cash Book is to mirror your bank statements.

When you have checked your bank statement to make sure that all transactions have been entered for the month, add up each of the columns. The sum of the 'Gross' column should be the same as the total of all other columns. If it is not, you should find the mistake and correct it before proceeding any further. Remember to file away your bank statements safely, in numerical order. Banks usually charge if they are asked to issue duplicate statements.

You now have the means to keep a careful check on your bank balance. Your Cash Book provides you with far more detail than your bank statements, and you will avoid the need to look back at cheque books or paying-in books if you want to check a certain transaction.

You can work out the Cash Book balance by subtracting your bank payments from the receipts. If this was your first month of trading, and you started from a £Nil bank balance, then this is the balance at the end of the month. For subsequent months, you will need to add the previous month's Cash Book balance to the current month's payments and receipts to arrive at the new month-end balance.

Finally, it is very useful to perform a 'bank reconciliation' at the end of each month. Remember that transactions which you have entered in the Cash Book for the month will not necessarily appear yet on the bank statement – cheques written on the last day of the month, for example, may not appear until the first week of the following month. It is important to check that the bank balance according to your Cash Book is the same, after you allow for timing differences, as the balance shown on the bank statement at the end of the month. You may already do this with your personal bank statements. It is equally important to do the exercise with your business bank account.

Cash expenses

As well as paying for overheads and expenses through your business bank account, it is likely that you will pay for items by cash (whether drawn out of your personal or business bank account), or by personal cheque or credit card. Obviously, if these are business expenses, you will want to incorporate them in your business records so that the picture of your business expenses is complete. The best way to keep track of these is to record them in a 'Cash Expenses Book'.

Your cash expenses are likely to include petrol, parking, postage, subsistence and so on. You should keep all documentation relating to these expenses, such as invoices or receipts, and mark each with a unique sequential number (e.g. C1, C2 etc.). File these in a 'Cash expenses' file in numerical order. Take care not to lose receipts and invoices – stapling petrol receipts to a sheet of A4 paper, for example, will help to ensure that you do not lose them.

You can enter details of these items in your Cash Expenses Book as follows:

Date	Description	Ref	Gross	VAT	Motor costs	Subsistence	Post/stny	Cleaning
5.1.95	Beech S/stn	C1	23.50	3.50	20.00			
7.1.95	Post Office	C2	19.00				19.00	
10.1.95	ABC Snacks	C3	2.35	0.35		2.00		
14.1.95	HPS Cleaning	C4	11.75	1.75				10.00
19.1.95	Beech S/stn	C5	21.15	3.15	18.00			
24.1.95	Post Office	C6	12.00				12.00	
JANUARY TOTAL			89.75	8.75	38.00	2.00	31.00	10.00

At the end of each month, add up each of the columns. The total of the 'Gross' column should be the same as the sum of the 'VAT' plus the analysis columns. If it is not, you have made a mistake, which you should correct before continuing.

Again, the headings for the analysis columns will vary, and should be based on the types of cash expenses you incur most frequently.

Together with your Purchase Day Book and Cash Book payments, your Cash Expenses Book provides you with a complete picture of all your business purchases, overheads and expenses. These will help to show you how the business is using its resources, as well as making it much easier for you to control your expenditure.

For many people who start up in business, the process of writing up books can seem alien, and initially of limited tangible benefit to the business. However, it is worth persevering. You will be providing yourself with a full record of the business's financial transactions, and as a result will find it much easier both to monitor how well the business is performing and to make financial decisions. Even if the volume of transactions is low in the early stages of the business, it is better to set up at the very beginning a simple system which can be expanded later, than to put off the exercise on the basis that it does not seem worth the effort at this stage. It may not be the most enjoyable aspect of running your business, but you might start to find it a more rewarding exercise than you expected.

Wages and salaries

If your business has employees, there is a statutory requirement for you to keep records of their pay and deductions of PAYE and National Insurance (this is covered in more detail in chapter 7). You should inform your local Inland Revenue office as soon as the business takes on employees; they will provide a 'New Employer's Starter Pack', which contains all the relevant forms and guidance with the calculation of deductions.

You will need to complete a 'Deductions sheet' every time employees are paid, so that you know the correct amount to pay them after PAYE and National Insurance deductions. All records including P45s, contracts of employment and so on must be kept safely. Do ensure that if the business takes on individuals who claim self-employed status you have evidence that this is the case.

Alternatively, for a business with a larger number of employees, it might be worthwhile investing in payroll software if the business already has a computer. A number of reputable packages are available.

> For example, a business with only seven employees found that processing the payroll each month had become relatively complex, because of varying tax codes, pension arrangements, bonus schemes and so on. The bookkeeper was afraid that errors could easily be made because of the number and type of adjustments required in the calculation of salaries and wages, in spite of her best efforts at accuracy. It was decided to purchase a payroll software package, so that (assuming she entered each employee's data accurately) the correct payroll calculations would be performed automatically by the software. This saved her not only considerable time each month, but also the worry that she might make arithmetical mistakes. Given the importance of the correct calculation of wages and salaries, this was a sensible decision

which allowed her more time to devote to other financial and administrative matters in the business.

Other uses of computer software as a business tool

Used sensibly, computers can make light work of certain tasks which might otherwise be awkward and time-consuming. However, you should consider various issues before making the decision to purchase computer hardware and software.

Does the business need a computer?

This will depend on various factors such as the type of functions which you require it to perform, the size of the business, and so on.

A 'one-man band' which provides an interior design service was considering purchasing a computer and software, but was unsure exactly how it would benefit the business. The number of financial transactions was relatively low, and quotations, bills and correspondence were prepared using a word processor. There were no other core functions which occupied any significant time, although the proprietor felt that a database would be rather smarter than the existing card index of customer details. However, this was not a major issue. Ultimately, he decided that to computerize any of these functions offered no particular benefits at this stage when it was weighed against the cost of the investment. He decided to review the situation in six months' time.

Cost

While a PC and basic business software can be purchased at a relatively low cost, a more sophisticated system may be a significant drain on the business's finances. You should therefore research the likely costs carefully, including any additional expenses such as installation, training, maintenance contracts and so on.

Staff skills

The computer literacy of those who intend to use the software should also be considered. There is no reason why any business person should not learn to use a range of software applications, even with no previous experience. However, there is no point in purchasing highly complex software with only a vague knowledge of how to operate it and no training, since this is likely to cause far more problems than it solves. Do not forget that you will inevitably have to invest more of your own time than you expect to become familiar with the software, however straightforward the package might be. It is tempting to imagine that once the computer is turned on and the software loaded you will be able to use it to its full advantage immediately. This is very rarely the case.

Software

It is not always necessary to purchase state-of-the-art hardware or software. Friends and business associates can be valuable sources of information about both hardware and software – and it may well be possible to benefit from their mistakes. Software is available for all types of business applications; it is important to consider in advance exactly what the business needs and will benefit from. For example, computer-aided office design software, which will assist in the design of office and workplace layouts, is not likely to be appropriate to a fish-and-chip shop.

Different businesses will have varying computer needs: those of a shop selling women's clothing will differ from a computer consultancy or a manufacturer of plastic bags. Any specific or unusual needs of the business should be identified first: Does the business need desk-top publishing software for mailshots? Or stock control software to monitor a large number of stock lines? Software is available to cover almost every imaginable business application, but you should consider seriously whether it will really benefit the running of your business. Do not forget that while sensibly chosen software used properly may help the business to run more smoothly, a poor choice used without proper thought and care will benefit nobody in the long term. Remember that the software should have a specific purpose as a business tool – and should not be used simply for its own sake.

Data Protection Act

The Data Protection Act exists to provide protection to individuals from the abuse of personal details about them which are held on computer systems. If, for example, you hold any data on your computer about individuals – even information such as addresses and telephone numbers – you must register under the Data Protection Act. The provisions of the Act are broad, so if you have or intend to purchase a computer, it is advisable to contact the Data Protection Registrar (telephone 01625 525777) to check whether your business needs to register. A fee will be charged, and registration lasts for three years before renewal is required.

Time management

Time management is a rather grandiose term for using your time as profitably as you can. This does not mean that you have to spend fourteen hours a day, six days a week managing your business, although from time to time there may be occasions when you do need to work long hours. It is very easy, especially in the early stages when you are full of enthusiasm, to feel that you have to devote all your waking hours to your new venture. It is equally easy to get priorities wrong: playing with a new computer rather than chasing customers whose payments are overdue. There will inevitably be days when your motivation is low and you do not work well, or problems keep arising which cause you frustrating delays. To balance this, there will also be days when you are full of energy, everything you do works to plan and you achieve far more than you had expected.

You can also take positive action to use your time as productively as possible. The demands on your time will inevitably be many and varied when you first set up your business – and will increase as the business starts to grow. It is important to ensure that you set aside sufficient time not only for dealing with customers, negotiating with suppliers and searching out new business, but also for the more mundane administrative tasks. Looking after the needs of customers or clients has to be a priority – without them, you would not have a business – but there is no point in clinching a large sale to a new customer if you do not also ensure that a sales invoice is sent to that customer promptly and payment is received on time. If you are new to running a business, this may be the first time that the structure of each working day and the tasks to be accomplished have been entirely your own responsibility.

There are some tasks which have to be dealt with as they crop up. For example, if a customer phones you and wants to discuss their next order, you will want to deal with the phone call immediately. There will be others which you can set aside for later or another day, such as sorting out your petrol receipts for the month. Yet others will be less easily allocated to a particular slot in the day, such as deciding on suitable computer hardware and software, or devising an appropriate stock-control system.

If you tend by character not to be particularly organized, then it is a good idea to set aside blocks of time for the completion of specific tasks. For example, you may choose to use Tuesday morning to raise sales invoices, sort out paperwork and write up your books. Some people find it helpful to block out time in their diary on a regular basis (say, half a day a week), and use this time to keep up to date with administrative tasks. A large diary, wall-planner or 'time system' organizer can be invaluable in assisting with time management. However, beware the temptation to fill a diary with well-intentioned plans which never come to fruition.

For most small businesses, and particularly those which require a high proportion of time to be spent away from the office base, it is simply a question of ensuring that a routine is established for:

- dealing with correspondence/customer enquiries;
- raising sales invoices and paying purchase invoices;
- sorting out cash expenses (especially petrol receipts);
- writing up books;
- chasing debtors;
- buying stocks;
- organizing employees;
- planning your advertising and marketing;
- etc.

The specific tasks will vary from business to business, as will the routine. Some tasks, such as chasing debtors, might demand only an hour or two each month. Others, such as dealing with correspondence, might require daily attention. Establish a routine at the outset; don't be forced into devising one later because the business is running out of control.

There will be occasions when emergencies arise – if staff fall sick, for example – and plans have to be rearranged. But if a business is basically well organized, the occasional disruption should not pose too serious a problem. In general, maintaining a good level of control over the general administration of the business will help to keep the business running smoothly and will help to free more time for the business's core activities.

5 Effective control and management

You are the person in charge of your business: you make the decisions, you control what happens and when. You may have previously had a key role in a business as an employee, but this is the first time that the entire running of a business is your sole responsibility. How you go about it in practice will depend to some degree on your own particular management style, but whatever your natural or chosen style, you will want to make sure that it is as effective as possible. If you have friends or associates who run their own successful businesses, do not ever be taken in by a claim that 'it runs itself': no business ever runs itself. What is probably closer to the truth is that they have put in a great deal of hard work to ensure that the business runs smoothly and is well controlled.

A brother and sister who run a small, family-owned manufacturing business were unprepared for the amount of time and emotional effort required to ensure that all aspects of the business are properly managed. They had both already gained management experience in demanding jobs, but find that taking responsibility for the successful running of an entire business needs their complete commitment. Each takes responsibility for specific areas of the business based on the skills and experience they had already developed, although they work with a high degree of consultation on all major issues. They both found it difficult to make the adjustment at first and admit to periods of doubt in the early stages about whether all their hard work was worthwhile. However, they have now built up a successful and well-run business which they find extremely rewarding, and feel that their initial efforts have more than paid off.

It is hard work, but do not be put off. While there are specific matters you will have to learn about, many of the principles of good business management are based on common sense and good communication; you will find this is reiterated throughout this chapter. Of course, there will be occasions when you make mistakes or misjudge a situation. This happens in all aspects of our lives, and while you cannot expect to be a perfect manager all of the time, you can learn valuable lessons from the problems and difficulties which arise to ensure that similar situations are handled better in the future.

This chapter looks at some of the financial, practical and personal aspects of understanding and managing a business, including:

- financial and cashflow control;
- what accounts can tell you;
- managing people, including your own management style.

Financial and cashflow control

If you have no previous experience of managing business finances, you may feel that there is little you can do to influence when money comes into or goes out of your business. However, there are a lot of practical steps you can take, none of which is difficult or complicated. The previous chapter stressed the importance of keeping accounting books and records which give you information about business performance, who owes the business what, and so on. Now you must use that information for the benefit of the business. You can make a difference to the financial position of the business by your active management of:

- debtors
- creditors
- bank account and cashflow control.

Debtors

The business's debtors are those who owe the business money. If yours is the type of business, such as a shop, in which your customers always pay you immediately, then you should not have problems collecting the money due to you from your sales. However, for the majority of businesses this will not be the case. Most businesses need first to send out a sales invoice, then wait for the customer to pay what is due. There can be a considerable delay between carrying out work or selling goods and receiving cash, but you can take steps to ensure that the delay is as short as possible.

First, it makes sense to send out sales invoices promptly. You might feel that your time is used more efficiently if you prepare and send out all your sales invoices for the month on the last day of the month. By doing so, you may be giving some customers three or four weeks' extra credit, and you will have to wait for your money for much longer than necessary. Depending on your business, try to prepare sales invoices as soon as work is completed or goods are sent out, or, if this is not possible, on a weekly basis. You should then be able to speed up the receipt of cash into the business.

A sole trader who runs a classic car restoration business ran into cashflow problems which he can now see were avoidable. He budgeted his overheads carefully and shopped around to achieve favourable prices for parts and spares. He also took great pride in his work, believing that its high quality would play a significant role in building up his reputation and hence his customer base. This was indeed the case, and he quickly built up a name for good craftsmanship and reliability. However, although he had plenty of work, he found that his bank account was always overdrawn. It transpired that he was in the habit of preparing invoices for his customers some considerable time after he had completed work for them, and then allowed them 30 days' credit. He claimed that the reason for this was pressure of work: he rarely had any available time for completing his paperwork. However, this meant that he had to pay his suppliers for parts and materials well before he received payment from his customers. The result was a bank overdraft he was never able to clear, including bank charges and interest he could ill afford. It was pointed out to him that the remedy was simple: ensure that when a customer collects a car, they are presented with an invoice immediately, with a request for payment within seven days. Although it took some time to achieve this discipline, he now manages to operate his bank account without any need for an overdraft facility.

You will also have to decide on credit terms for your customers, if any. It may be customary in your type of business to request payment when the order is received, or when the goods are released or the work completed. If this is the case, you should not suffer the problems of long outstanding invoices. However, for most businesses, customers will expect free credit, and you will have to decide whether your credit terms are, for example, 7 days, 30 days or 60 days. This should be stated on the invoice, together with any other terms and conditions which apply.

To encourage speedy payment, you might consider offering a prompt payment discount. This means that if customers pay within the specified period, they are entitled to deduct a percentage from the value of the invoice. The benefits of offering discounts are not clear-cut, since:

- it is not proven whether discounts are effective at persuading customers to pay promptly;
- customers may take the discount but still not comply with the credit terms.

Conversely, you might consider charging interest on outstanding invoices. If you do choose this option, then you should state it in the terms and conditions on the sales invoice. For example: 'The right is reserved to charge interest on outstanding invoices at 1.5 per cent per month.' This is probably of most use when the monetary value of invoices is relatively high, or if customers are persistently late in paying. If invoices are low in value, you may find that your time is more productively spent phoning the customer to chase payment than in preparing an additional very small invoice for the interest charge.

If you are carrying out work which will span a relatively long period of time, you might consider charging a non-refundable deposit. This serves two purposes:

- you will incur costs while you are carrying out the work, and the deposit will ensure that you are not entirely out of pocket during the period;
- it will serve as a form of insurance against the recovery of at least part of your costs.

You will soon find that an effective system of credit control is essential. To start with, you can request credit references from new customers, or pay a credit agency to check their creditworthiness before you offer credit terms. Once you have sent out your sales invoices, you should be able to tell from your sales accounting records (see chapter 4) when they fall due, and which customers need to be chased for payment. Debt chasing is a task that many people find difficult at first, but you should nevertheless make it part of your monthly routine. If you do not, some customers may recognize this and stretch credit terms for as long as they can because they know you will not be chasing for payment.

A phone call is often more effective than a letter in the first instance. You can ask whether any problem exists with the overdue invoice, and, if not, politely ask when you can expect to receive payment. It may be useful to incorporate in the terms and conditions on the invoice a sentence such as: 'Any dispute with the content of an invoice should be notified in writing to XYZ Ltd within seven days of its delivery. If no dispute is raised, the invoice is deemed to be accepted.' This should help to reduce the likelihood of a 'dispute' being used as a stalling tactic by slow-paying customers.

If a customer tells you that 'a cheque is in the post', ask exactly when it was posted, the amount of the cheque and which of your invoices it refers to. If you are told that 'the bookkeeper is on holiday', 'there's nobody in the office who can sign a cheque', etc., ask (again, politely) when the bookkeeper is returning, or when somebody will be available to sign cheques. Phone again on the appropriate day. Above all, do not be put off. There is no point in chasing two or three times, only to give up through frustration. Again, this should also help you to avoid falling victim to the more obvious stalling tactics.

There may be occasions when your efforts are still not productive and you are forced to resort to legal action. It is surprising how many slow payers write a cheque immediately if they receive a formal letter threatening to issue a writ or to start bankruptcy or winding-up proceedings. Do not be tempted to use it as an idle threat, but do be prepared to take the appropriate action where necessary. Your local County Court can supply you with details of the necessary paperwork, or you might consider using a solicitor to assist you in your first case.

It is easy, if you do not review your debtors regularly, to allow the amount of money you are owed to increase to a worrying level, particularly if you have a high volume of low-value invoices. You need to demonstrate to your customers that even if you are prepared to be sympathetic in desperate cases, you always expect prompt payment in normal circumstances.

Creditors

At any time, your business will almost inevitably owe money to various creditors, who might include suppliers of goods and services, HM Customs and Excise for VAT, a finance company for finance lease repayments, the Inland Revenue for income tax and National Insurance, and so on. Many small businesses rely heavily on trade credit, without which it would be necessary to pay for goods and services on receipt, if not before. For a small business in its infancy, the effect on its bank account could lead to a need for far greater levels of bank borrowing. Trade credit, of course, is free of charge whereas bank borrowing can be subject to substantial charges and interest.

Many people, either in their personal or business dealings, have abused suppliers' credit terms in some small way, from not paying the telephone bill until the final demand arrives to ignoring a phone call from an irate supplier. However, this should not be generally regarded as a good financial management policy, nor as good practice. Indeed, you would be extremely foolish to ignore the stipulations regarding payment made by bodies such as HM Customs and Excise or the Inland Revenue. Their powers to recover debts are considerable and they will levy stiff penalties and interest for late or non-payment of outstanding liabilities.

This does not imply that it is in order to ignore the payment terms of other businesses and bodies who wield less power: other creditors do have recourse to legal action to collect their debts.

In order to keep track of the amounts you owe to suppliers of goods and services, you need to keep a record of the purchases you make on credit (see chapter 4). This will enable you to see which invoices you have paid and which are outstanding, and will help you to assess which suppliers need to be paid. Of course, this will depend to some degree upon how much the business can afford to pay out. If, for example, you are waiting for a substantial cheque from a customer which is overdue, you may find that you cannot pay your suppliers without exceeding your overdraft limit. In such a case, good communication is vital. You either need to speak to your bank manager to explain the situation and ask that your cheques will be honoured, or speak to your suppliers and explain your request for an additional period of credit.

If you are suffering cashflow difficulties and your bank will not permit you an overdraft (or allow you to extend an existing one), negotiation with your suppliers is essential. Most businesses are prepared to make reasonble allowances if only their debtors are honest with them. You might, for example, offer to pay part of an invoice now and the balance in two weeks' time. Provided you honour the agreement, your creditors will probably be perfectly amenable to your suggestion. If you are unable to honour the agreement, you must contact your supplier again to explain this. In these situations, the worst action you can take is to do nothing. Any relationship of trust which has developed will instantly be destroyed, and you may find your supplier demands, say, cash on delivery in the future as a result.

Some businesses choose to pay suppliers of goods and services which are directly related to sales only when they receive payment from their own customers.

A public relations agency generated considerable bad feeling with their suppliers of printing and other media services by refusing to pay for work until they had passed on the costs to their clients and received payment. This led to delays in some cases of several months. Although the agency always met its liabilities eventually, a number of suppliers began to refuse to carry out any additional work until the backlog of invoices had been paid. The partners of the agency admitted that they would not tolerate this type of policy from their own customers and agreed to rethink their payment terms. However, they now had to work hard to rebuild the goodwill which had originally existed with their suppliers.

On the other hand, there is no need to pay every invoice as soon as it arrives. If a supplier offers 30 days' credit, then take it. Your own business's bank balance will benefit as a result.

Bank account and cashflow control

You may feel, in common with many other small and young businesses, that your control over your bank account is severely curtailed by the behaviour and demands of your debtors and creditors. If you have problems collecting what is owed to you by your customers, and at the same time your suppliers are demanding payment, then you may feel relatively powerless to exercise satisfactory control over what is paid into and out of your bank account. The worst course of action is to abandon responsibility and cease to take notice of your business's bank balance. It is important that if you do suffer cashflow problems, then you are the first to be aware of the fact.

It is always a good idea to take steps to establish a good relationship with your bankers, however small your business may be. For example, you might talk to your bank manager about major developments in the business and keep him or her informed about trading results. It is equally important to highlight potential cashflow problems as soon as you are aware of them: a bank is more likely to be sympathetic if forewarned about a business's problems than if overdraft limits are simply breached without notice. The latter will also be a more expensive option in the long term: the cost of letters regarding breached overdraft limits and the resulting bank charges should be an avoidable expense. The embarrassment of bounced cheques and the potential loss of reputation could also be damaging to the business overall. Remember as well that bank overdrafts are generally repayable on demand. In normal circumstances if a business operates within its overdraft limit, then the bank should not have cause to demand repayment of its money. However, if bank letters are persistently ignored and an overdraft limit constantly exceeded, then this could ultimately be the result – and could easily lead to the collapse of the business, not to mention the personal financial and emotional distress of the individuals involved.

Similarly, if your bank requests regular information about the business's trading performance, discuss how you can best provide it. It may seem unimportant to you, but as in all your business dealings, it is advisable not to ignore requests from those who can have such a significant influence over your business. The same applies to letters and phone calls from your bank, which should always be dealt with as soon as possible.

An owner of a small engineering business which specialized in work for motor racing teams learnt that good communication with his bankers was essential. His work was seasonal in nature, with a very busy period from spring to autumn followed by a severe drop in work during the winter months. His bank account fluctuated accordingly. After his bankers began to express concern that his overdraft was increasing steadily during the second winter of trading, he contacted his bank manager to explain in more detail the reasons for the fluctuations and his expectations for trading the following year. The bank was entirely satisfied with his explanations and happy to continue to support the business, but requested quarterly meetings to review progress. In retrospect, he admits that he could have pre-empted the situation by providing the bank with this information much sooner.

The day-to-day management of your bank account can be helped by taking some simple steps to control it. It is not sensible, for example, to have a number of separate cheque books in circulation with different individuals within the business, all with authority to write cheques as they feel is appropriate. It will inevitably be extremely difficult to keep track of the bank balance at any time. If possible, use only one cheque book, under the control of one person. You might also choose to require that cheques are signed by two authorized persons rather than just one. This may not always be practical if yours is the type of business where a high proportion of time is spent away from the business base. However, you must devise some means of ensuring that control is maintained over the writing of cheques, however large or small they might be.

It can also be helpful to keep a running note of the bank balance on your cheque stubs: in order to be accurate, you will have to keep track of all non-cheque payments out of the bank account as well as amounts paid in. This can be a useful discipline, and should help to ensure that you are not caught out when you write a large cheque only to find that there are insufficient funds in your account. Asking your branch to send you bank statements weekly will also help you to monitor the movements on your bank account.

If you do not keep a note of your bank balance in your cheque book then it is important to check on the balance by performing a regular bank reconciliation (this is discussed in chapter 4). Remember that although your bank statement might indicate that you have adequate funds available to meet your immediate requirements, there may be cheques which you have written but which have not yet cleared the bank account. Conversely, the same applies to amounts paid in. It is therefore essential to keep a check on the 'actual' bank balance after these items have been taken account of.

On another level, you can also ensure that major items of expenditure are planned for and not undertaken on a whim. Make sure that you budget for large, one-off purchases. It is easy to feel that the business is secure today and can afford the expenditure, only to find that it is unable to pay suppliers next month as a result.

Look also at spreading the cash outlay on major purchases by means of hire purchase or finance lease agreements. An interest charge will be included in the monthly repayments, so that the total expenditure will be greater than if the item were purchased outright. However, the benefit to the business of spreading the cash outflow may outweigh the interest charge. Alternatively, you may choose to pay a substantial deposit with, say, 50 per cent of the total cost repaid via hire purchase.

Since you can't operate your business without adequate banking facilities, it is a matter of common sense to ensure that your bank account is controlled as effectively as possible. Your contact with your bank manager may be minimal when the business is progressing well and you have no particular financial difficulties. However, when you do need help, you will want the support of your bank: this will be more easily achieved if you have taken the trouble to establish a satisfactory relationship beforehand.

What accounts can tell you

The vast majority of people have no need to interpret or even look at a set of accounts until they are in business themselves. It is therefore not surprising that many business owners have difficulty 'reading' their own business's accounts, although it is often assumed that this is a skill they somehow acquire simply from being in business.

Accounts themselves are frequently regarded as a necessary evil, required for the purposes of working out how much tax is due to the Inland Revenue, and in the case of limited companies, for filing at Companies House. While a set of accounts may not make ideal light reading, they do provide a business with fundamental information about its performance and financial stability. Again, it is a matter of common sense to try to understand and use that information rather than filing the accounts away as an incomprehensible and largely useless document.

The amount of detail in the form of pages of notes and background information which is included in a set of accounts will vary from business to business: the accounts of a major listed company will be more complex than those of a self-employed electrician. However, there are two 'statements' which will almost invariably be included:

- profit and loss account
- balance sheet.

For some very small businesses, it is sometimes the case that only an 'Income and expediture' account is prepared, which is similar in form and content to a profit and loss account.

Profit and loss account

The profit and loss account is a statement of the business's trading performance for (usually) one year and its purpose is to determine the level of profit or loss made by the business for the year.

It includes the turnover for the year, less all the expenses which relate to that turnover. These expenses are split between direct costs (such as materials and labour which are directly attributable to sales) and indirect costs (such as administration and property costs which are incurred regardless of the level of sales). In the case of a limited company, it will also include other items such as dividends and corporation tax, which affect the profit made by the business.

A set of accounts will usually include figures for the previous year as well, so that the reader can make comparisons and determine trends within the business. A profit and loss account for a sole trader or partnership might take the following form:

J. E. Broadwood Consultant
Profit and loss account
Year ended 30 April 199Y

	Note	Year 30.4.9Y £	£	Year 30.4.9X £	£
Sales			87,628		62,790
Cost of Sales:					
Opening work in progress		(270)		(417)	
Closing work in progress		956		270	
Direct costs		(2,037)		(1,017)	
			(1,351)		(1,164)
Gross profit			86,277		61,626
Overheads					
Salaries		13,804		10,000	
Employer's National Insurance		1,078		815	
Training		350		294	
Motor vehicle expenses		4,809		4,982	
Printing, postage, stationery		1,086		1,312	
Advertising and marketing		1,796		1,034	
Computer consumables and maintenance		431		519	
Subscriptions		577		571	
Books and publications		820		683	
Data protection registration		–		75	
Accountancy		800		750	
Legal and professional		260		130	
Bank charges		240		235	
Insurance		756		690	
Repairs and renewals		315		76	
Telephone		706		651	
Electricity		75		87	
Travel		168		123	
Subsistence		12		14	
Entertaining		340		270	
Bad debt charge	5	1,427		1,486	
Sundry expenses	6	304		312	
Bank interest		--		2	
Hire purchase interest		–		192	
Fixed asset disposal		–		(91)	
Depreciation	1	3,473		3,745	
			(33,627)		(28,957)
			52,650		32,669
Interest received			1,849		1,847
Net profit for period			£54,499		£34,516

If the business were a limited company, figures for corporation tax and any dividends paid or payable would also be included before arriving at the 'Net profit'. Neither of these are applicable to a sole trader or a partnership, so they are not included here. Additionally, the terminology used and the layout of the profit and loss account would be slightly different, as formally required by the Companies Act. However, the overall content would be broadly the same.

What does the profit and loss account reveal about the business? The left-hand column gives the trading results for the current year, with last year's results in the right-hand column. First, there has been growth in sales from £62,790 to £87,628, an increase of some 40 per cent. On its own, this cannot tell us whether the business has necessarily enjoyed a corresponding increase in profits, but in this case net profits have indeed grown by nearly 57 per cent, from £34,516 to £54,499. It therefore follows that direct costs and overheads have been well controlled, and the increase of £4,670 in overheads is largely accounted for by an increase in salaries and employer's National Insurance. There are no major fluctuations between the two years in any overhead items. The overall picture at this stage, is of a small business which has enjoyed healthy growth this year. Of course, a clearer picture can always be gained by looking at accounts for a number of years rather than just two.

The column headed 'Note' refers the reader to additional information in the accounts, which will provide the reader with extra details about certain items in the accounts. A great deal of additional information can be gained by referring to the notes.

Balance sheet

A business's balance sheet is a 'snapshot' of its assets and liabilities. This means that it summarizes, at a given date, all that the business owns and all that it owes.

A balance sheet for the same sole trader will be in a form similar to the following:

J. E. Broadwood Consultant
Balance sheet
30 April 199Y

	Note	30 April 199Y £	£	30 April 199X £	£
FIXED ASSETS					
Tangible fixed assets	1	2,439		5,876	
Investments		10,000		–	
			12,439		5,876
CURRENT ASSETS					
Work in progress		956		270	
Debtors		8,555		8,458	
Prepayments	2	829		750	
Bank deposit account		78,527		53,305	
		88,867		62,783	
CURRENT LIABILITIES					
Bank current account		836		732	
Purchase ledger		498		655	
Other creditors and accruals	3	2,571		1,614	
Hire purchase creditor		1,115		1,230	
Value Added Tax		5,581		3,250	
		10,601		7,481	
NET CURRENT ASSETS			78,266		55,302
LONG-TERM LIABILITIES					
Hire purchase creditor			963		2,408
			£89,742		£58,770
REPRESENTED BY:					
PROPRIETOR S CURRENT ACCOUNT	4		£89,742		£58,770

The assets (what the business owns) in the balance sheet for J. E. Broadwood are split into two categories. Fixed assets might include motor vehicles, plant and machinery equipment, and investments. Current assets are those such as debtors, stocks and positive bank balances: as a general rule, either cash or items which are readily converted into cash.

Liabilities (what the business owes) are also split into different categories. First, there are current liabilities, which are the amounts that the business must theoretically pay within one year of the date of the balance sheet. These will include items such as a bank overdraft, trade suppliers, HM Customs and Excise for VAT, amounts due on hire purchase agreements and so on. Long-term liabilities include amounts which are due after more than one year, and might include items such as part of a bank loan account or part of a hire purchase creditor.

What information does the balance sheet give about the business? There are two figures which you can look at to gain a first impression of the stability of the business. The first is the amount for net current assets. This is arrived at by subtracting current liabilities from current assets. If the current liabilities are greater than the current assets, the figure will be negative, and becomes net current liabilities. This figure tells us whether in the short term the business owns more than it owes or vice versa. In the example below, it can be seen that the business has ample 'current' resources to cover its financial commitments to suppliers and other parties who are owed money. However, if the figure were negative, it would mean that the business owed £78,266 more in current liabilities then it had the current assets to cover.

The second figure to look at is the balance sheet total, in this case £89,742 for the current year. This indicates that if the business were liquidated at the balance sheet date, then theoretically it should realize nearly £90,000 after it had paid all its suppliers and other creditors, received money from its customers, sold its fixed assets and so on. Of course, the figure will not be this precise in practice, but the balance sheet total nonetheless provides a basic guide.

In both cases, it is useful to compare the figures with those for the previous year, to find out whether the financial stability of the business is improving or deteriorating.

This balance sheet is for a sole trader, and hence the bottom 'half' shows the proprietor's 'current account', which is also £89,742. This figure comprises:

- the accumulated profit or loss made by the business to date (not just for the current year);
- any money drawn out of the business for personal use by the proprietor during the year;
- any money introduced into the business by the proprietor personally during the year. As well as sums of cash this could also include, for example, business expenses which have been paid for personally by the proprietor.

If the business were a partnership, then the proprietor's current account would be replaced by the partners' current account. The constituent elements would be exactly the same, except that amounts drawn out of or introduced into the business would be included for all of the partners, rather than just one individual.

For a limited company, the propietor's current account would be replaced by 'share capital and reserves'. As the name suggests, this comprises:

- the paid-up share capital of the company;
- the company's accumulated profit or loss to date;
- any other 'reserves' (although the profit and loss account is usually the main 'reserve').

Again, the column headed 'Note' refers the reader to extra information about certain items in the accounts. For a limited company, the additional details which have to be included are prescribed by the Companies Act. For a sole trader or a partnership there is more flexibility.

Do look at your own accounts carefully, and if they contain items which you do not fully understand ask your accountant to explain them to you. Don't be afraid that you will look foolish – it is vital that you, as the business owner, understand how your business is progressing.

Managing people

You may already have worked in jobs in which part of your role was the management of other individuals or a team of people. Perhaps you were also responsible for liaising with other businesses or individuals outside the firm. If this is the case, you will already have valuable management experience. On the other hand, you may have little or no such experience and feel unsure about your management capabilities.

In either case, you will need to deal effectively with a variety of people on a number of different levels. This is a vital part of the management of your new business. The people you are likely to have most frequent contact with in the daily running of your business will include:

- your staff
- customers
- suppliers.

Just as importantly, you will also have to manage yourself.

It is worth reiterating that a good and effective management style generally owes much to the application of common sense and good communication. Of course you will make mistakes or errors of judgement from time to time, and it is important both to admit to them and to learn from them. Nobody expects you to be perfect – but you will still have to work to ensure that problems which arise are avoided in the future.

This section is not primarily concerned with management theory, but rather aims to set out some guidelines to help the smooth running of your business. Nobody can teach you how to manage your business, but you can take steps which will help you to stay in control and to derive as much satisfaction as possible from your venture.

Staff

Your relationship with individual members of your staff will depend to some extent on the number you employ. If you work with just one or two others, you should be able to develop a close working relationship. If the numbers are larger, you may have to delegate much of the day-to-day supervisory responsibility. In either case, your aim is to build up a team of people who work productively and effectively together. Although good working relationships are developed over a period of time, you can take steps to maximize the contribution of staff to your business.

It is important to define individual employees' responsibilities and objectives clearly. If people do not fully understand what is expected of them in their work, they will inevitably feel less comfortable in their job and be less able to perform at their best. If you prefer work to be carried out in a particular way, make this clear: it will save time and misunderstanding later.

Employees should be helped to understand their own responsibilities and objectives and how they will be met. You may prefer simply to give an employee a list of tasks, either in writing or verbally, with no further explanation as to which are important or urgent, how they would be best achieved, and so on. In some jobs this may be practical, but in most circumstances it is more helpful for the employee if they understand how their work fits into the business overall, why it is important and how and when they are expected to carry out the work allocated to them. A little time spent in discussion can also help to provide motivation and make work more satisfying.

Try to determine employees' particular strengths and weaknesses, so that work can be allocated appropriately. For example, an employee whose strength lies in selling may not be the right person to help with writing up the books. On the other hand, they may have previous bookkeeping experience and be the ideal person. You need to consider the practical skills which employees have gained in previous jobs, other abilities they have developed which are linked with activities outside work, and personal qualities which you become aware of as you come to know the employee better. For example, a sociable and articulate employee might be better suited to accompanying you to a trade fair at which you hope to promote your business than another employee who is by nature shy and retiring.

Be prepared to *listen* to your employees' ideas – remember that they may have experience which complements yours. Make it known that you are open to suggestions, and that even if you do not always act upon them, you are prepared to listen to and discuss new ideas or methods. Employees might have good ideas which they have gained from previous jobs, or ideas for carrying out work more effectively. Conversely, if you make changes which affect an employee's work, consult them and ask for their comments.

It is always a good idea to keep employees informed and to share good as well as bad news. You are more likely to develop loyalty to your business if an employee feels they are an important part of it.

Much has been written on the subject of managing staff and how best to motivate them. However, common sense and an open-minded approach will provide you with a good basis for a productive working relationship with your staff.

Customers

Obviously, your relationship with your customers or clients is crucial to the success of your business. You want to encourage repeat business and hope they will recommend your product or service to other potential customers. Even if you do fall out with a customer, try to ensure that your approach and attitude remain polite, however difficult this may be: you do not want to develop a reputation for a lack of courtesy, even if a dispute is in progress.

What steps can you take to manage your relationship with your customers? It may be useful to put yourself in the position of your customer and ask yourself how you would like to be treated. Obviously there will be specific matters which depend on the type of business you are running: a solicitor will have to take account of factors which do not apply to a bookshop or a decorator, and vice versa. But the basic principles are the same.

Deal with enquiries by phone or in person from customers as fully and courteously as possible. If you delegate responsibility for handling enquiries, ensure that those employees have sufficient training and information available to do their job effectively. If you or they are unable to deal with the enquiry immediately through lack of information or because the appropriate person in the organization is not available, it is always better to offer to phone the potential customer later than to try to bluff. Make sure that the customer is contacted again as soon as possible.

While carrying out work for a customer, discuss with them progress and any problems which arise. Be realistic about the time needed to carry out the work and about your own commitments. Do not tell a customer you can carry out work tomorrow or next week when you know this will be impossible to achieve: there is a vast difference between putting in long hours to satisfy your customers' deadlines and being completely unrealistic about the amount of work you or your staff can complete within a given time-scale. Again, be honest with your customers. Try to prioritize work so that deadlines can be met comfortably. But when problems do arise and deadlines become impossible to meet, contact your customer immediately to explain the problem and to give a realistic estimate of the completion date.

A business run by two partners which provided corporate hospitality services found it was losing business because clients became dissatisfied with a lack of consultation. Although the events organized by the business were run efficiently and generally passed off smoothly, the partners tended to change arrangements requested by clients – either because of cost or because the partners felt their ideas were better – but failed to inform clients of the changes before the event took place. They assumed that because they were the 'experts' and had years of experience in this field, clients would be happy to accept their superior judgement (as they saw it). They began to receive complaints, not because of the quality of their service *per se* but because clients felt they could not rely upon the business to follow their specific instructions. In a number of cases, clients stated that they might well have taken the advice of the 'experts', if only they had been consulted.

There may be other specific points which apply to your own dealings with your customers, and these too are likely to be based on common sense, honesty, courtesy and good communication. Remember that although the quality, reliability and so on of your product or service are of prime importance, your *treatment* of your customers can make a significant difference to the success of your business.

Suppliers

In your relationship with your suppliers, you are the party dictating your business's needs for goods and services. At first you may feel overwhelmed by the number of alternative suppliers who all appear to be able to meet your requirements. It is worthwhile spending time carrying out some research, first to define your exact needs and then to find suppliers who can match those criteria as closely as possible. Whether you are researching suppliers of raw materials for manufacturing purposes or of stationery, you can ask yourself the following questions:

- How important is price?
- What discounts are available?
- Will the supplier offer trade credit, or will they demand cash on order or delivery?
- What is the lead time (the time between order and delivery)?
- Can they deliver overnight in an emergency?
- How important is the quality of the product or service? For example, you may need top quality materials to manufacture your product, but you may need only medium quality stationery.
- Do you want to try to support other small local businesses? Is this feasible?
- Does the supplier have any reputation for reliability, quality, speed of delivery?

- Can business associates provide any recommendations?

It is important that you make your requirements clear to your chosen suppliers, and establish whether they are able to satisfy them. As a new customer to them, they may ask you to provide credit references before offering you trade credit. For some businesses, this is now standard practice and not a reflection on your particular business.

What if you experience problems with a supplier who consistently sends you faulty goods or repeatedly fails to deliver on time? Some people find it very difficult to make a complaint and others have no compunction about taking a fairly aggressive stand. Whatever your personal style, you are the customer and therefore entitled to expect the quality of product or service for which you are paying. It is important that you make your views known, since your suppliers' shortcomings could in turn cause you difficulties satisfying your own customers' requirements or orders. However, unless the circumstances are extreme, a polite and restrained approach which sets out your complaint in clear terms will usually achieve better results than plain abuse.

Your suppliers are important to your business; however small a customer you may be, they should take your business needs seriously. You may find you have to experiment before you find those which best suit your needs, but it is worth persevering for the sake of the benefits they can bring your business.

Yourself

Developing a management style which contributes positively to the smooth and successful running of your business will take time, even if you have previous experience of managing projects or a team of people or a department. You will have to take responsibility for all aspects of the business, even if you have little or no experience in certain areas. Poor management is certainly one of the major contributory factors in business failures, although it is equally true that even the best managers will struggle to create a thriving business from a badly made product or a poorly executed service.

Human behaviour is not an exact science, and it would not be realistic to try to construct an exhaustive list of management Do's and Don'ts. However, in more general terms, there are traps which you can avoid falling into and styles of management which can be more destructive than beneficial to your business.

Lack of effective communication is a relatively common problem in businesses of all types. It might occur because you, as the business owner-manager, want to retain as much control over the business as possible. You may therefore feel that if you strictly limit the information you pass on to your employees they will be unable to challenge your position of authority. In a small business – indeed in any business – this is unlikely to be the most productive approach. There is obviously no need to give every employee full details of every aspect of the business all of the time. However, when a business comprises a small team of people, they are likely to be more enthusiastic and motivated about the business if they feel they are a useful part of it. For example, if a job has to be completed urgently, explain why. If the business has had a particularly successful month, say so. If it has had a difficult six months and is facing problems in the longer term, explain the measures you are taking to try to improve the business's stability.

Lack of business management experience is hardly a fault, but it is an obstacle that has to be overcome by the owners of many new businesses. It can have serious implications if bad decisions are made because of a lack of understanding of the consequences or of the underlying information. You will inevitably learn a great deal about business management in a short time, if you are prepared to be open-minded and receptive. It is still important to recognize your weaknesses and to be prepared to listen to advice from other sources, be they experts or specialists, or business associates who have experienced similar circumstances. Trying to pretend to yourself and others that you are more experienced and knowledgeable than you actually are will not benefit your business in the long term. It may be difficult to swallow your pride and admit that you need support or help, but it is likely to produce far more positive results.

A domineering attitude towards business management is also unlikely to produce positive results. You may feel that since you are in charge, you are the only person who should have any influence on how the business is managed. This does not necessarily imply an overbearing or aggressive attitude; it might mean that the suggestions and ideas of staff and colleagues are simply ignored. Again, this is likely to be connected with a desire to remain in absolute control of the business. When the business is in its infancy, it may be that you are operating it alone, and have no choice but to take all decisions yourself. As the business grows, an approach which involves the delegation of tasks and responsibility to suitable staff, and sensible consultation on important decisions with those who are sufficiently experienced to make a useful contribution, will probably yield greater benefits for the business.

The propietor of a village store learnt that his staff could contribute more than he had appreciated to the success of his business. He left the day-to-day running of the shop to an assistant, although he continued to take sole responsibility for deciding what type of goods the shop would stock and for purchasing them. His assistant made suggestions on numerous occasions for new lines which could be stocked, based on requests she received from clientele. However, the proprietor refused to pay attention to her ideas, believing that he was completely in touch with the needs of his clients. It was only when he had lost a number of regular customers to a rival shop that he began to appreciate the value of his assistant's advice and realize that since she was dealing directly with the customers, her knowledge might be better than his. Fortunately he acknowledged his error before the shop suffered irreparably, and is now able to admit the value of her contribution to the success of his business.

Maintaining a sense of perspective is also vital for anyone running their own business. If the business is experiencing difficulties – perhaps a major customer has been lost, or the bank has refused to increase an overdraft limit – it can be very easy to lose sight of everything but those difficulties. Your business is of course a very important part of your life, and you may depend on it entirely for your income. If you employ staff, a feeling of responsibility towards them will add to your problems. Depending on your temperament, you may be able to cope calmly or you may feel your problems are overwhelming: the majority of people fall into the latter category at some stage. The most constructive and helpful action you can take is to *talk*, perhaps to a trusted friend or associate and to your partner or family. Remember that they will be affected by your business and will not thank you in the longer term if you keep business problems hidden from them. Just as importantly, you need an outlet outside the business to relieve the stress caused by any business problems. Again, it may be difficult at first to admit that the business is not progressing as smoothly as you would like, but you are unlikely to derive any benefit either for yourself or your business by suffering in silence.

In spite of the problems which arise, managing your own business can be extremely satisfying. Allow yourself time to gain experience and develop your approach; try to learn as much as possible both from your successes and from the mistakes you make.

6 Taxation

When confronted by issues related to tax, the reaction of many people is often one either of boredom or of fear. As a business owner, you are probably interested primarily in how much tax you will have to pay and when you will have to pay it, and less concerned about the intricacies of how it is calculated. You may feel that since your accountant will sort out your tax affairs, there is no need for you to devote your time and energy getting to grips with them. This is entirely understandable, but it is nevertheless useful to have some background knowledge of the various taxes which will apply to your business and a general idea of how they are worked out. Additionally, you may decide that it makes more sense for you to deal yourself with matters related to, for example, VAT and PAYE on the earnings of employees and directors. You need to have a good grasp of how they operate so that you can apply them correctly.

The types of tax which are most likely to apply to your business are:

- Value Added Tax (VAT);
- income tax and National Insurance payable on employees' salaries and, in the case of limited companies, directors' remuneration;
- income tax and National Insurance payable on the profits of the business, if you are running a sole trade or a partnership;
- corporation tax payable on the profits of the business if you are running a limited company.

Value Added Tax

Value Added Tax is a tax on expenditure, and for this reason it is known as an indirect tax. It is collected on behalf of the government by all VAT-registered persons (a person is registered for VAT purposes, not a business).

The tax is split between:

- output VAT, which is the VAT you charge on your sales (known as 'supplies');
- input VAT, which is the VAT you reclaim on your business purchases.

There are three different classifications of goods and services for VAT purposes:

- standard-rated, which means that VAT is charged on goods and services at (currently) 17.5 per cent;
- zero-rated, which means that although VAT is charged theoretically the rate charged is actually 0 per cent;
- exempt, which means that no VAT is charged.

Your accountant or adviser will be able to tell you which of the categories your business falls into, or whether more than one classification will apply to you.

The *basic* principle of VAT is a simple one. If you are VAT registered and you supply standard- or zero-rated goods or services to your customers, you have to pay over any VAT you charge – the 'output VAT' – to HM Customs and Excise. Similarly, you reclaim from Customs and Excise the VAT that has been charged to you on your *business* purchases – the 'input VAT'. You are sent a VAT return to complete, usually quarterly, on which you enter the amount of output VAT you have charged and the input VAT you are reclaiming for the period; the difference between the two is either payable to or refundable from Customs and Excise.

Until you have completed a VAT return and can see for yourself how it works, this may all seem complex and rather daunting. However, with some initial guidance from a professional adviser, most owners of small businesses find that they are able to deal with their VAT returns themselves if they keep adequate bookkeeping records.

For example, two partners run a public relations consultancy. Their supplies are standard-rated, which means that they charge VAT on their sales invoices at 17.5 per cent of the net invoice total. At the end of their VAT quarter, they work out from their accounting records that the total VAT they have charged in the three-month period on their sales invoices is £3,500: this is their figure for output VAT. The VAT they have suffered on their business purchases and which they can reclaim amount to £1,700: this is their input VAT. The amount they pay is therefore:

	Output VAT charged	3,500
less:	Input VAT suffered	1,700
	Amount payable	£1,800

You should be able to work out your output and input VAT from your accounting books and records (see chapter 4). You may find it useful to look back at the examples in that chapter to see where you would enter your output VAT and input VAT. The output VAT is entered in the VAT column of the Sales Day Book – the VAT charged on sales. The input VAT is entered in the three books which contain details of business purchases –

the VAT columns of the Purchase Day Book, the Cash Expenses Book and the Cash Book. Even if the accounting books you keep are slightly different from those described here, the principle will be the same.

You must keep all the books and records which support your VAT calculations for six years. This means not only your accounting books, but also all of your invoices, receipts, bank statements and so on. Additionally, in order to reclaim VAT on your business purchases, you must have a VAT invoice or receipt. This does not necessarily mean that it will show all the details of the VAT charged to you, but it *must* show the VAT registration number of the supplier. For example, if you buy petrol for business purposes, ask specifically for a VAT receipt otherwise the receipt you are given may not be sufficient for VAT purposes. Remember that you cannot reclaim VAT on zero-rated or exempt purchases, such as postage or financial services.

Keeping good accounting records means that when you have to complete your VAT returns, you should be able to work out your basic output and input VAT figures with relative ease. However, before you fill in your first VAT return, it is a good idea to consult your accountant to make sure that your figures are accurate and complete: the example above has necessarily been simplified for the purposes of illustration. It is also possible that you will have to make adjustments to your figures for items such as the private usage element of the business petrol you have purchased or of home telephone or mobile phone bills which are paid by the business. This is because you can reclaim VAT only on the *business* element of your purchases. You will find it easier to establish these matters as early as possible, to avoid confusion and the accumulation of errors later on. You should also check that there are no special rules which apply to your business and which could affect your VAT calculations.

It is essential that VAT returns are completed accurately and submitted together with the payment within the given deadline – one month after the end of the VAT quarter or month end. A progressive system of default surcharges exists for the late payment of VAT – and the Finance Act 1985 states clearly that 'an insufficiency of funds to pay any tax is not a reasonable excuse'. Similarly, a system of penalties exists for serious and persistent 'misdeclarations' of VAT (i.e. errors on your VAT returns).

VAT is in fact a highly complex tax, with many apparent contradictions: for example, some foodstuffs are standard-rated and others are zero-rated. It is important when you set up your business to establish the specific VAT implications which apply to you. There are many exceptions to what appear to be straightforward regulations and it is in your interests to ensure that you deal with VAT correctly from the outset. Remember that your local VAT office will always be happy to provide you with advice and guidance.

VAT registration

COMPULSORY REGISTRATION

If your business makes annual taxable supplies (which means standard-rated or zero-rated sales) in excess of the VAT registration threshold, then you *must* apply for VAT registration. The term 'annual' does not refer to a calendar year or to the business's accounting year, but to a 'rolling' twelve-month total. The threshold is usually increased annually by the Chancellor of the Exchequer in the Budget. To work out whether you are approaching the registration threshold, you will need a record of your sales each month.

It is important to notify your local VAT office of your need to be registered for VAT within thirty days of the end of the relevant month, otherwise you may have to pay a penalty. Additionally, be aware that both standard-rated and zero-rated supplies must be included in the twelve-month total. This means that even if you make some sales on which you would charge VAT at 0 per cent, you still include them in your twelve-month total.

There are some cases where VAT registration may be disadvantageous to the business.

The proprietor of a takeaway pizza shop finds that she must register for VAT because her sales for the last twelve months exceed the current limit of £46,000. This means that she must now charge VAT at the standard rate of 17.5 per cent on her pizza sales. However, she does not feel that it is possible for her to add 17.5 per cent to her selling prices because she knows that her clientele would not accept that increase. For most businesses that sell goods or services to other VAT-registered businesses this does not present a problem, because their customers are themselves able to reclaim the VAT charged to them. However, individual consumers are not able to reclaim any VAT which they are charged and are therefore far more 'price sensitive'. To add to the proprietor's problems, most of the stock she purchases is zero-rated, so she is able to reclaim only a small amount of input VAT to offset against her output VAT. While she is not happy with this situation from a commercial point of view, she realizes that she has no alternative but to register for VAT.

VOLUNTARY REGISTRATION

You may decide that it is advantageous to the business to register for VAT from the beginning, whether or not your taxable supplies are expected to reach the VAT registration threshold. This might be the case if you are making standard-rated supplies to other VAT registered customers, who can in turn reclaim that VAT. Your customers will not lose out as a result of the additional 17.5 per cent charged to them and you will be able to reclaim the VAT you suffer on your business purchases.

If you apply for voluntary registration, HM Customs and Excise have to be satisfied that a business is being carried on, and that taxable supplies have been or will be made before they will register you for VAT. They will need some evidence of your intention to make taxable supplies, if you have not already made any. This evidence might take the form of a sales order, or alternatively, invoices for the purchase of supplies or equipment for the business will normally suffice if you do not have any documentation relating directly to sales yet.

You will need to fill in a VAT Application for Registration form (Form VAT 1) and send it to your local VAT office. In due course, the business's Certificate of Registration will be issued, which gives details of the business's VAT number, the date of registration and the dates at which VAT returns are to be prepared.

Income tax and National Insurance

Income tax is known as a direct tax because it is directly related either to the amount you earn as an employee or director, or to the amount of profit generated by a sole trader or partnership. (A limited company pays corporation tax on its profits, rather than income tax.) National Insurance contributions are calculated in a similar progressive way on earnings and profits over a certain threshold.

Income tax and National Insurance on salaries and directors' remuneration

When you take on an employee to whom you pay a salary which is greater than the Lower Earnings Limit (even if it is a member of your family) or if you are paid remuneration as the director of a company, you become responsible for calculating and deducting the correct amounts of income tax (PAYE) and National Insurance from those salaries and paying them over to the Inland Revenue.

If you are a sole trader or a partnership, you should tell your local Inland Revenue office as soon as you take on an employee. If you are trading as a limited company you should tell them as soon as the company is set up. They will send you a package of forms and booklets called a 'New

Employer's Starter Pack'. The package will give you guidance on how to calculate deductions of PAYE and Class 1 National Insurance. It will also tell you what you should do with your new employee's P45, and what to do if your new employee does not have a P45.

When you first look at the New Employer's Starter Pack you may feel daunted by the volume of information it gives you. The majority of small business owners quickly learn how to deal with salaries and deductions, but do not be afraid to ask your professional adviser for guidance if you feel unsure at first.

Income tax and National Insurance on the profits of sole traders

Before you can be treated as a sole trader for tax purposes, the Inland Revenue and Department of Social Security must be satisfied that you are in fact self-employed. For most sole traders, this will not even arise as a questionable issue, but there are some for whom it may be less clear. For example, you work as a 'self-employed' consultant:

- for only one client;
- at your client's premises;
- using your client's equipment;
- within your client's normal office hours;
- taking your instructions directly from your client's employees.

If this is the case, your status as a self-employed individual is likely to be called into question. This is because you do not fulfil the basic criteria (as listed above) which will be applied to determine whether you are self-employed or, in fact, effectively an employee.

Other criteria which may be applied include:

- whether you are obliged to carry out your work yourself, in person, or are free to use others who are chosen and paid by you;
- whether you control how, when and where you carry out your work;
- whether you put right errors or re-do work in your own time and bear the consequences when things go wrong.

These criteria are known as 'Badges of Trade'. If you can demonstrate to the Inland Revenue and Department of Social Security that you satisfy their criteria, then you should have no problem in achieving self-employed status in their eyes.

How is your tax calculated?

The exact calculation of a business's tax liability will vary from business to business, so it is not really possible to give more than a broad outline here.

The amount of tax you pay on your sole trade will be based on the amount of profit you make. However, your business profits as shown by your accounts will rarely be the same figure as the profits on which your tax liability is calculated. This is because certain adjustments have to be made to your business profits in order to arrive at the 'taxable profits' figure.

For example, there are certain business expenses which you will correctly include in your accounts, but which are not allowable for tax purposes, such as depreciation of fixed assets, business entertaining and provisions for bad debts. Conversely, you will exclude income such as bank interest on which tax is paid separately, so that you do not pay tax on it twice. Any amounts you take out of the business for your personal living expenses are not included when calculating your profit.

You may also have made some capital expenditure during the period, purchasing a car or plant and equipment, for example. Although you cannot treat this expenditure as a business expense in the same way as, say, business telephone bills, you should be able to claim a form of tax relief known as Capital Allowances. The Capital Allowances you can claim will depend on the rate in force for that type of asset, when the expenditure occurred and other factors. The most common allowance is the 'writing down allowance', which is similar to a depreciation charge on motor vehicles, plant and machinery, equipment and so on. However, there are many other rules which govern different types of asset and how they are treated. Capital Allowances do not apply if you are renting or leasing cars or equipment; the cost to the business in this case would be treated as an ordinary business expense.

Class 4 National Insurance will also be calculated on your taxable profits, if they exceed a certain limit, at a rate of 6.3 per cent. There is also an upper limit beyond which you pay no further contributions. Class 4 National Insurance is paid at the same time as your income tax.

When do you pay your tax?

In the past, sole traders have paid their tax and National Insurance on what is known as the 'preceding year basis'. This means that if you had an accounting year-end of 31 December, then after the first few years of trading (when special rules apply) your tax bill for the fiscal year ending on 5 April 1995 would be based on the profits you had earned in the accounting year which ended on 31 December 1993. There is therefore a delay of fifteen months between when the profit is earned and when it is assessed for tax purposes.

With effect from the tax year ending on 5 April 1998, this will change and sole traders will be taxed on the 'current year basis'. This means that the profits for the accounting year ending on 31 December 1997 will form the basis for the tax bill for the fiscal year ending on 5 April 1998. The 'current year basis' simply means that the tax bill for a given fiscal year is based on the profits earned in the accounting period which ends in that fiscal year.

The deadline for submitting your tax computations will normally be 31 January, nine months after the end of the fiscal year, and penalties will be automatically levied for late submission.

The system for the payment of your tax is also being revised. Up to the fiscal year ending 5 April 1998 payments are made in two equal instalments, on 1 January and 1 July following the fiscal year end. This means that using the first example above, you would pay the tax on your profits for the accounting year ended 31 December 1993 on 1 January 1995 and 1 July 1995.

Under the new system, the dates on which tax is paid and the system under which it is calculated are both changed. The new system is known as 'Self Assessment'.

First, any capital gains tax is payable on 31 January following the tax year in which the gain arose. For all income, including profits, you will make two payments 'on account', followed by a 'balancing' payment. This will be necessary because the two payments on account will be based on the tax liability of the *previous* year (since we do not yet know the current year's results). The first two payments will each be 50 per cent of the tax liability on all sources of income for the previous year. The first payment will be made on 31 January in the tax year, and the second on 31 July following the end of the tax year. When the 'actual' results for the current year are known and the tax liability can be calculated accurately, it will then be possible to work out how much tax has been overpaid or underpaid, and the balance will be paid when the tax return is submitted on 31 January the following year.

For example, in 1996/97 Jill has a tax liability of £8,000. In 1997/98 her tax liability is £8,900 and she also has capital gains of £16,000 which led to a further liability of £6,200. The payments she makes for 1997/98 are as follows:

31.1.98	50% x £8,000 (based on previous year)			= £4,000
31.7.98	50% x £8,000 (based on previous year)			= £4,000
31.1.99	Income tax actually due	8,900		
	Less: Income tax paid	8,000		
	Balance payable		900	
	Capital Gains Tax due		6,200	
	Total payable			= £7,100

This example is simplified to illustrate the principle. In each year, the payment on 1 January will be made up of the first instalment for the current year *plus* the balance for the previous year.

Obviously, it is not possible to switch from one system to another overnight; 1996/97 is the transitional year in which existing businesses move from the old basis to the new.

What if you make losses?

If your sole trade makes losses rather than profits, you can potentially make use of them by offsetting them against other income or profits which you make. You may be able to reduce the amount of tax you pay on other income or profits by claiming a 'refund' of tax on your losses. This may either mean that you receive a refund of tax, or that you reduce the amount of tax you would otherwise have paid on other sources of income. This works as follows:

- you can carry back losses to offset against other income in the previous year, as long as you were carrying out your sole trade in that year;
- you can offset losses against other sources of income in the current year;
- you can carry losses forward *ad infinitum* to offset them against future profits from the same trade.

Very importantly, in the first four years of your sole trade, you can 'carry back' losses to offset them against any other sources of income in the *past* three years. This can have significant consequences for your cash flow.

Derek has set up in business as a sole trader. In the fiscal year 1995/96, he has tax losses of £10,000. He is able to carry back those losses to offset against his income of £50,000 in the fiscal year 1992/93, three years ago. He was paying tax in 1992/93 at a rate of 40 per cent. The amount of tax he can reclaim is therefore:

$$£10,000 \times 40\% \qquad = £4,000.$$

This makes a significant difference to his cashflow, and is especially valuable in his early years of trading. He also receives a repayment supplement from the Inland Revenue, which is a form of interest based on official interest rates.

If he had not had sufficient income in the fiscal year 1992/93 to use up his losses, then he would have gone forward to the next fiscal year, 1993/94, and offset the balance against his income for that year.

Once the income for a given year has been used up in this way, no further claims can be made for that year!

Class 2 National Insurance

As a self-employed individual you will also pay Class 2 National Insurance contributions, which used to be known as the 'stamp' because you could buy stamps over the counter at the Post Office. If your earnings are beneath a certain low level, you can claim exception from the Department of Social Security from the need to pay: your accountant will be able to help you to determine whether this applies to you. The level of Class 2 contributions is a fixed weekly amount which you can pay monthly by direct debit or by quarterly bill.

Income tax and National Insurance on the profits of partnerships

The tax and Class 4 National Insurance liabilities of a partnership are worked out in a similar way to a sole trader, the difference being that the liability is split between the partners. Again, any amounts drawn out of the partnership for the partners' personal use are not included in the profit calculation. The changes in the 'basis' periods which apply to a sole trader also apply to a partnership, but with some further fundamental changes to the way partnership tax is treated.

From 1996/97 onwards, partnerships will be sent tax returns on which they report not only the income of the partnership, but also how the profit is shared between the partners. For all partnerships which are set up after 5 April 1994, the partners will effectively be treated as sole traders within the partnership. This will also apply to existing partnerships from 1997/98, and should lead to a simplification in partnership tax.

The rules which apply to the use of losses and to Class 2 National Insurance contributions also apply to partnerships.

Corporation tax on the profits of limited companies

Limited companies pay corporation tax, not income tax. There are two rates of corporation tax: the reduced 'small company' rate of 25 per cent and the full rate of 33 per cent. The rate at which you pay will depend on the level of profits made by the company.

The amount of tax the company pays will be based on various elements, including:

- its level of profits or losses;
- whether it has 'chargeable gains' from the disposal of capital assets;
- whether it has investment income;
- how much it claims in capital allowances.

There are other factors which can affect corporation tax, and it is advisable to consult an expert to do your calculations.

Profits are worked out in a similar way to those of sole traders and partnerships, except that any salary you take as a director will be included as a business expense, unlike the drawings of sole traders and partnerships. Directors' salaries are treated as a business expense in the same way as other salaries in arriving at a taxable profit figure. If the company has made a profit, it may be worth increasing the amount paid to you in salary as a director, if the tax and National Insurance on that salary will be less than the corporation tax on the company's profits. However, this can be a complex calculation, and you should ask your accountant's advice since there may be other factors which affect your decision.

The system for paying corporation tax is a simple one, and is known as 'Pay and File'. A company must pay its estimated corporation tax within nine months and one day of the end of its accounting year – after which interest charges and penalties are levied. It must also file its corporation tax return, normally within twelve months of the end of the accounting year. Sometimes it may not be possible for a company to work out accurately its corporation tax liability by the time payment is due, so the payment will have to be estimated. If it later emerges that the first payment was not sufficient, the company can make a further payment to the Inland Revenue at any time, in order to avoid additional interest charges.

If a company makes losses or has no corporation tax to pay, it must still complete the corporation tax return.

As with income tax, it is important to know that if your company makes losses, these can be used as follows:

- to be carried back up to three years to offset against chargeable profits, so long as the same trade was being carried on in those years;
- to use in the current year to offset against other profits;
- to be carried forward ad infinitum, to offset against profits from the same trade.

Whatever your business, dealing with taxes is not an issue you can ignore. It is a good idea to have a basic idea of how they work, even if you are not interested in the finer points. Paying your tax bills is not optional, and the sensible business owner will try to budget in advance: if you know you have to pay £5,000 on 31 January next year, try to start putting aside money well before that date, perhaps in a separate bank account. When it is time to pay the bill, it will come as less of a financial shock than if you simply hope that your bank account will have sufficient funds in it.

7 Progressing

As a business owner, it is often assumed that you know how to cope with a whole range of issues related to your business, from dealing with bankers to employing staff. If you are new to running your own business, there is not necessarily any reason why you should be knowledgeable about such matters, although you may have gained some useful experience in your previous jobs. You cannot be expected to become an expert overnight in fields in which you have only limited experience and expertise, and it is not advisable to convince either yourself or third parties otherwise. You will probably find that you can achieve far more by:

- drawing on the experience of friends and associates in business;
- using specialists when you need expert assistance;
- making use of sources of information such as guidance booklets produced by professional and government bodies.

This chapter looks at some of the issues which commonly arise when a business is in its infancy:

- finding premises;
- organizing insurance;
- employing staff;
- promoting your business;
- using patents and trademarks to protect your product.

Some may not apply to your business until you have been trading for a while and the business has grown significantly. Others may be relevant from the beginning, or they may arise on a number of occasions during the life of the business as it grows and develops. It is a disparate group of topics, but often these are areas in which business owner-managers have little or no experience, but which are vital to the smooth running and success of the business. For example, a business which misjudges or fails to recognize its staff requirements could find its mistake expensive both financially and in the additional difficulties involved in running the business if it emerges that the 'wrong' person has been chosen for the job.

Premises

What sort of premises?

The type of premises you need to run your business may be obvious to you from the start. On the other hand, you might first have to make the decision whether you need premises separate from your home at all. You may have very specific needs, or may be able to be very flexible.

If you are a manufacturer, then unless you are working as a 'cottage industry', making your product on the kitchen table or in the garage, you will need to find suitable workshop, factory or industrial premises. For a retail business, there will probably be no option but to look for suitable shop premises. If you are providing a service, the space you need, at least initially, may be very limited. Perhaps you spend most of your time at your customers' own premises, for example, if you repair washing machines, or perhaps you are a courier who is away from the business base for most of the day. In many cases, the amount of space you will need may be limited to a table where you can do your paperwork.

If you do need to find premises, you will first have to define your needs:

- How much space do you need?
- How important is geographical location?
- Are there any environmental factors, such as noise or pollution, which will restrict your choice? For example, if you need to operate a heavy goods vehicle, you will have to apply to the local council for a licence and show that you are trading from suitable premises.
- What facilities do you need, such as storage or warehouse space, parking or lorry access, adjoining office space?
- Do the premises need good transport access for clients?
- How important is appearance? For example, do you need space in a purpose-built office complex, or is a converted office over a high street shop adequate?
- What facilities do you need, such as access to conference or meeting rooms, separate reception area, own entrance, kitchen?
- What amenities do you need? What sort of heating and lighting? Would you prefer air-conditioning, security system, phone system and so on to be installed already?
- How much can you afford to pay?

You may not find premises which match up precisely to all of your criteria, but do not be tempted to compromise too much. If a factory is only just big enough now, you are likely to outgrow it fast. Your search will, however, be made much easier if you work out beforehand roughly what you are looking for.

If geographical location is not important, you might consider looking for assistance under various government schemes. English Estates (0191 487 8941) provides industrial and commercial property in the Assisted Areas of England on flexible terms, sometimes with simple tenancy agreements. It will also build or alter premises to meet firms' specific needs. There are also some twenty Enterprise Zones in the UK which are exempt from rates and which are almost free of planning controls. Additionally, 100 per cent Capital Allowances are available on the construction or extension of property within the zones. The Department of the Environment can provide you with details of these zones (0171 276 4603).

In English rural development areas, the Rural Development Commission (01722 336255) provides small workshop units, either direct to the business or in partnership with local authorities. The Commission also provides grants for converting redundant buildings, loan facilities for general premises and advice on general planning matters.

You might also try contacting your local authority to see if they maintain a register of vacant commercial property or managed workshop units within their area, and to see if any schemes are available to help new businesses. Local newspapers and estate agents are the other main sources of information. It is worthwhile looking around local industrial estates and business parks, especially when the property market is sluggish. You may well find that industrial and office units are available at much reduced rents, or with a rent-free initial period.

Whether you are buying a freehold or a lease, you will need to have a survey carried out on premises. The Royal Institute of Chartered Surveyors (0171 222 7000) can provide you with names of surveyors in your area, or you can look in your local *Yellow Pages* or ask around for personal recommendations. It may be tempting to avoid the expense of a survey, particularly if the premises you have in mind are relatively new and appear to be in a good state of repair. However, the one-off cost now could save you far greater expenses, not to mention legal battles and heartache, later.

A small business which relocated from rather cramped office conditions to newer, purpose-built ones had chosen their new premises partly because of the extensive storage space available in the basement. Since they generated a large quantity of paperwork which had to be retained, this seemed ideal. They did not bother with a survey, and it was not until the following winter when the basement flooded, destroying many of their files, that they realized that serious problems existed. Whether a survey would have revealed this particular problem is not known, but they believe now that it might well have alerted them to the fact that the premises had flooded previously.

If you take out a lease, you should check its terms carefully, and it is advisable for your solicitor to assist you. You should establish the length of the lease, whether there are any restrictions on the usage of the premises which might affect you, who is responsible for repairs and renewals, what are the proposals for rent reviews, who is selling the lease and whether a lease premium is payable, and so on. Ask your solicitor for detailed guidance.

Use of home as office

If you are providing a service, such as some form of consultancy, training, teaching or other specialist or professional skill, it may be possible for you to work from home, especially if the space you require is limited and one room can be set aside to be used solely for your business.

There may be restrictions on using your home as business premises, such as restrictive covenants on the land (you can check this with your solicitor) and you may need to obtain planning permission from your local authority if you significantly change the use of the land and premises. You will also need to consult your insurance broker: your household insurance may be invalidated if it is not suitably amended to take account of your business activity. If you are claiming some of the costs of running your home as business expenses, there also exists a potential liability to Capital Gains Tax when you sell the house. This is unlikely to occur unless you use the house solely for business purposes, but it is as well to check the current situation with your accountant.

Quite apart from legal and regulatory restrictions, you should also consider whether you are temperamentally suited to working from home. It has the advantages of avoiding the cost of renting or purchasing alternative premises, the cost of travel to work, and so on. However, some people find it very difficult to work effectively in their own home, either because they become distracted by domestic matters or because they simply do not feel that they are 'at work'. Conversely, others find it difficult to switch off at the end of the day and feel that their personal life is disrupted to an intolerable extent.

If customers or clients will visit you at home, you will also need to consider the importance of the impression that your 'office' will create. In some circumstances it may be relatively unimportant. In others it may be crucial to create a particular impression very quickly, and you should consider whether you can achieve this by working from home.

A consultant in the early stages of planning and setting up her own business was uncertain whether to opt for the additional expense of office premises or the cheaper but less glamorous option of converting her spare bedroom into an office. She wanted to keep her overhead costs as low as possible in the first period of trading, but had always worked in large, modern and sophisticated offices which she had assumed were essential to the success of a business. However, she anticipated spending a large proportion of her time at clients' premises. After discussion with a former colleague who had started his own business, she came to the conclusion that she could create a perfectly business-like and adequate office at home through a relatively small financial outlay on computer equipment and second-hand office furniture. She was very enthusiastic about her business, and expected to experience no problems motivating herself to work at home.

Two years on, she believes she made the right decision, since she has made valuable savings in her overheads. However, she is aware that at some stage she will outgrow her current office, and with this in mind she keeps up to date with the local commercial property market.

Local authority regulations

You must check that your premises have the planning permission appropriate for your business. If not, you will have to apply to your local authority planning department to change its use. Even if there are no objections, the process can take some months. You can obtain a leaflet, 'A Step-by-Step Guide to Planning Permission for Small Businesses' from your local authority.

Similarly, if you plan to make structural alterations, you should consult the local authority planning and building regulations departments, the Water and Sewerage Undertakers and the County Council Fire Authority to ensure that your plans conform to their requirements.

The Health and Safety implications of your business activity must be investigated at an early stage as well. You will probably have legal responsibilities to comply with Health and Safety regulations if you employ people in a workshop or factory, and need to register your business either with the Local Health and Safety Executive (for most factories and workshops) or the local authority (for most offices, shops and catering businesses).

If you are a manufacturer whose processes lead to any emissions, either to the air, land or water, then you need to check with the local authority Environmental Health Department whether authorization is needed. The same applies if food is being stored, prepared or served on your premises.

You also need to check whether the premises need a fire certificate, and if so, whether one is already in place. You can apply to the Fire Authority of your county council to check.

For certain types of business, such as the sale of alcohol or weapons, hotels, heavy goods operators, mobile shops, nursing homes and employment agencies (this is only a limited list of examples), you may need a licence or some other form of authorization to operate. Although licences are issued by a number of different authorities, contact the licensing sections of your local authority in the first instance.

Searching for premises and dealing with the regulations and requirements which apply to the business will almost inevitably take longer than you expect. You may become frustrated and tempted to cut corners in order to save time and costs. This is understandable, but highly inadvisable. Of course you want to get your business started as soon as possible and avoid any unnecessary delays, but you may later pay the price if you don't take seriously the conditions which have to be satisfied before you can move into your new business base.

Insurance

Deciding what types of insurance cover your business needs, obtaining quotes and filling in proposal forms may not be interesting tasks, but trading without appropriate and adequate insurance cover is a risk you can't afford to take.

There are several ways of purchasing insurance:

- from an insurance company representative;
- from your bank;
- from an insurance broker.

In theory, an insurance broker may be the best option, since they are less likely to be tied to selling only the insurance offered by their own company. However, if a business associate or friend particularly recommends a company representative, do include them on your list. The British Insurance and Investment Brokers Association (telephone 0171 623 9043) will be able to suggest some brokers who deal with small businesses, or you may prefer to shop around locally.

Depending on the type of business you are running, there are various classes of insurance which you may require:

- **Employer's Liability Insurance** You must have this by law if you have any employees. This will cover accidents to your employees in the workplace as a result of their work or in the course of it, and you must display a current certificate of insurance in the workplace.

- **Public Liability/Product Liability Insurance** This covers members of the public who suffer injury while at your premises or as the result of using your product.

- **Motor Insurance** You must have this by law for all of the business's vehicles. Even if you are running a business on your own from home, you must tell your insurer that you are using the vehicle for business purposes or any claim you make may be invalid. It may be wise to insure against fire and theft as well as taking out the minimum third-party insurance.

- **Building and Contents** These should be covered against disasters such as fire, flood, burglary and so on. Ensure that stocks of goods are also covered, as well as any that might be held at other premises. Some types of equipment require specific insurance.

- **Goods-in-transit Insurance** This covers goods whilst they are transported to or from your suppliers and customers, for shipment abroad, for repair and so on, either in your own vehicle or by some other form of delivery. If you are involved in the regular transport of goods, it is probably worthwhile taking out goods-in-transit insurance.

- **Consequential Loss Insurance** This covers you against the continuing costs of your business after a disaster so that, for example, you are able to pay for alternative premises and wages after your office has burnt down.

- **Professional Indemnity Insurance** This is compulsory for certain types of work, particularly where you are providing clients with expert advice. It covers you for claims against you for damages which result from misconduct or negligence. In an increasingly litigious society, you would be well advised to consider some form of indemnity insurance, even if it is not required by your professional or trade association.

- **Keyman Insurance** This is most appropriate where the business is run by one or a small number of individuals, whose death would cause losses to the business.

- **Loss of Money Insurance** This covers you against the theft of cash, cheques and so on from your premises, while in transit, from employees and from your home. If you are running a retail business and regularly have substantial sums of cash on the premises, this may be worthwhile.

- **Personal Insurance** Disability and health insurance, life insurance etc. should also be considered, in case of personal disasters which make it impossible for you to continue your business. The extent of the insurance will vary according to your personal circumstances, but do not ignore the fact that some insurance is essential.

Staff

You may need to take on staff from day one or you may be able to operate your business alone for some time, perhaps with support from your family who can offer particular skills which you do not have. Alternatively, you may be undecided whether you need employees, either part-time or full-time to help you deal with specific areas of your business, perhaps with administration and bookkeeping or marketing and selling.

It is a difficult decision to make, especially if you feel that the extra financial cost is relatively large in proportion to the business as a whole. For example, a despatch rider working alone will probably find it more economical to buy a mobile phone and answerphone than to employ someone full-time to answer the phone and take messages at the business base.

However, for many businesses additional staff will be essential, or may become necessary as the business grows and you can no longer manage to run it single-handed. Deciding when it is appropriate to take on staff can itself be difficult: you have to balance the extra benefit to the business against the extra costs. You need to make sure that you take on staff who can make a tangible difference to the running of the business, either in terms of the additional skills they bring, or the extra time they allow you to concentrate on, for example, developing and improving your product or building up a more extensive customer base.

If you do plan to run your business entirely single-handed, are you sure that you have both the time and the skills to do so? If not, think about the areas in which part-time or bought-in *ad hoc* support would be of most value to you: there may be circumstances where buying in services is a more economical option. Remember that the cost of employing someone is likely to be greater than just the amount of wages or salary you pay. You must budget as well for your Employer's National Insurance contributions, and perhaps sick pay, holiday pay and pension contributions. You may also need to buy additional office equipment, tools, car or van, motor insurance, and so on.

The proprietor of a small business buying and selling second-hand industrial machinery found that he was able to manage his business very effectively single-handed with the help of specialist support services. He knew that his strengths lay in his negotiating and selling skills, and decided he would concentrate his efforts where they were of most benefit to the business: on buying and selling machinery. He bought in the services of engineers to overhaul the machinery where necessary, a self-employed administrator for one day each week to keep his paperwork and correspondence under control, a firm of accountants to keep his books and prepare monthly management reports and a telephone answering service to take calls when he was away from the office. Of course, all of these services had to be paid for each month, but he calculated that it was more profitable for him to concentrate on buying and selling and thus generating more business, than to devote time to the other tasks at which he was less skilled and save the fees he was charged.

Before you can start advertising for suitable staff, your first task will be to define who you are looking for. You will need to ask yourself the following questions:

- In what areas do you most need support?
- How many staff do you need?
- What tasks will they carry out?
- Do they need to have any special qualifications, previous training or experience?
- Are you able to provide sufficient training yourself, where appropriate?
- How much do you envisage paying your staff?

How much you pay your staff will depend on various factors, and you should consider:

- How much can you afford to pay?
- What is offered for similar posts in similar businesses?
- Is a combination of basic salary and commission or bonus appropriate?
- Do any trade union agreements affect what you pay?

If you decide to employ the services of someone who is self-employed, be aware that the Inland Revenue and Contributions Agency may decide that they are in fact your employee, if they work solely for you at your business location. If this is the case, you will be liable for their PAYE and National Insurance contributions.

Being an employer

When you take on staff, you also take on a number of responsibilities. There is a wealth of information available for employers in booklets produced by the Department of Employment, the Inland Revenue and the Department of Social Security, as well by bodies such as the Equal Opportunities Commission, the Commission for Racial Equality, ACAS, and the Health and Safety Executive.

In particular, the series of leaflets published by the Department of Employment covers a comprehensive range of topics on employment legislation and employee rights, and should be available from your Local

Employment Service Jobcentre. ACAS also produces a very useful handbook, *Employing People – A Handbook for Small Firms*, as well as a series of advisory leaflets.

Terms of employment

When you take on an employee who works for you for more than sixteen hours a week, you must give them a written statement, within 13 weeks of the date their employment begins. This statement will set out:

- name of employer and employee;
- job title or description;
- date employment begins, and period of employment if it is not permanent;
- rate of pay and how it is calculated, if appropriate;
- how and when the employee will be paid – monthly, weekly etc.;
- hours of work;
- holiday entitlement, including arrangements for public holidays and holiday pay, if appropriate;
- arrangements for sickness and injury, including any sick pay;
- arrangements for pensions and pension schemes, and whether a contracting-out certificate under the Social Security Pensions Act 1975 exists which applies to the employee;
- notice periods for employer and employee;
- details of disciplinary and grievance procedures if the business, together with any associated businesses, has more than 20 employees.

There are other terms which you may want to incorporate in the statement, and the Employment Department leaflet 1 'Written statement of main terms and conditions of employment PL700' sets these out in full.

It often happens that these points are set out in a letter offering the job to the employee. If that is the case, they do not need to be covered again in a written statement.

If an employee works for you for between eight and sixteen hours a week, then you are not required – although you may choose – to give them a written statement until you have employed them for five years. If an employee works for you for less than eight hours a week, then they have very limited rights as an employee, and you are not required to give them any form of statement setting out their terms and conditions of employment. Again, you may choose to do so.

Induction

To help an employee settle into a new job comfortably and adjust to their new routine, some form of induction process is a good idea. This basically refers to the process of making a new employee familiar with the business, the job itself, other staff, and so on. Some businesses have structured programs which include specific training sessions. If yours is a very small business, the process will probably be more informal, but should still include:

- administrative details, such as signing terms of employment and dealing with P45;
- general familiarization, including more details about the business, introduction to other staff and location of amenities;
- specific details about the job itself: where the employee will work, what tasks they are expected to carry out and when, any necessary training and who to ask for guidance and help.

A new employee will settle in faster and more easily if they are clear about what is expected of them and feel confident that they understand the specific tasks they are to perform. You will also be able to build a productive working relationship more quickly if good communication is established at the very beginning. It is worth stressing that the benefit of good communication to all parties – employee, employer and the business overall – should never be underestimated.

The proprietor of a transport business decided to take on someone part-time to help with general administration and bookkeeping, since he could no longer manage all the work himself. The new employee had the right experience and skills, had previously worked in small businesses and had excellent references. Given her obvious abilities, the proprietor assumed she would simply know what to do, and gave her only the minimum explanation of how the business worked and what tasks she was expected to deal with. He then left her alone in the office for most of her working hours, while he tried to seek out new business. After a month, it was clear that while some of her work was done to a very high standard, other tasks appeared to be completely neglected. The database had not been updated for jobs done that month, nor had any of the bookkeeping (also computerized) been started.

It transpired that since she worked only part-time, she had been leaving messages for the proprietor asking for guidance on these tasks. He had not paid them any attention, and she was therefore unable to carry out her work. Eventually, she asked to arrange a meeting, in which they could discuss a solution to her difficulties.

When they discussed these issues, the proprietor was horrified that he could have overlooked such a fundamental problem. He had been so accustomed to working on his own that he simply failed to see that a new employee would need some training.

To prevent similar problems in the future, they arranged that they would have a formal discussion each week about the tasks which needed completing and how the business was performing generally. Once this problem was overcome, they succeeded in working together very effectively, but both acknowledge that effective communication is absolutely essential.

Pay

By law, you have to provide an itemized pay statement each time an employee is paid. This sets out:

- gross wages or salary;
- deductions, and the reasons why amounts are deducted (e.g. PAYE, NIC, pension contributions, and so on);
- net wages or salary, and method of payment.

You must inform your local Inland Revenue Office as soon as you take on an employee who is paid more than the Lower Earnings Limit. If you have previously not had any employees, they will send you a New Employer's Starter Pack, which contains details of the records you must keep, how to calculate deductions of PAYE and National Insurance, and how to deal with Statutory Sick Pay and Statutory Maternity Pay.

Health and Safety

The Health and Safety at Work Act 1974 requires that both employers and the self-employed provide a safe working environment, both for themselves and for visitors and customers. If a business has more than five employees, then a written health and safety policy must be in place. Equally, employees have a duty to take reasonable care of themselves and of other employees at work.

In recent years, additional legislation has been put in place in the UK following directives from the EC.

The Employment Department booklets 'Don't wait until an inspector calls' and 'Essentials of health and safety at work' and the ACAS Advisory Booklet 'Health and Employment' provide useful guidance on aspects of health and safety at work.

Welfare

It is important to realize, particularly in a small business where every employee is a key employee, that personal and emotional problems do arise which will affect an employee's performance at work. Although you as an employer are not primarily responsible for the 'non-work' problems of your staff, as a fellow human being you can offer your support. Problems can arise in various areas, such as bereavement, divorce, illness, finance and drugs, amongst others. Some problems may need professional help, and you can provide support by allowing reasonable time off to attend consultations, meetings, self-help groups, and so on.

The employee may also feel reluctant to discuss their problem with you, for fear that you will be worried about the effect it has on their work. It will be more beneficial for all concerned to demonstrate your support and to help your employee to resolve their problem.

It can be difficult to make the adjustment to employing staff, especially if you have been accustomed to working alone. You now have the responsibility for providing someone else with work, for ensuring you work together effectively, and for their well-being as an employee. However, if you choose the right person at the right time, the rewards will far outweigh the burden of the responsibilities.

A surveyor who had worked on his own for several years with some *ad hoc* support from his partner, reluctantly decided he needed to take on someone to help him cope with his growing workload. He was very uncertain about how well he would adjust to working with a colleague again, and took extreme care over recruitment on the basis that working effectively together was as important as the employee's technical skills. Six months later, he feels his priorities were proved right. He feels able to trust his employee absolutely, and has complete faith both in her skills and her integrity. It has made a huge difference to him to share the problems as well as the workload of the business, which continues to grow successfully and profitably.

Promoting your business

Promoting your business is not simply a question of advertising. There are many other ways in which you can convey a particular impression of your business. For example:

- the image which you and your staff project;
- the manner in which you handle enquiries or telephone calls;
- the quality and appearance of your letterhead or packaging;
- the promptness and efficiency with which you deal with customers' orders.

This alone will not necessarily win you new business, but it will help to build up an impression that customers and other third parties associate with your business.

You might also find out about local business associations that you can join to build up your network of business contacts. Businesses talk to each other, they ask for recommendations and discuss their experiences with suppliers, and so on. The more people who are aware of the existence of your business, the better chance you have of expanding your customer base.

You will also want to devise some means of advertising your business on a broader scale. If you have no previous experience of using different forms of advertising to promote a product or service, deciding how and where to advertise may not be immediately obvious. You will want to convey the right impression and you will want it to reach the right people. There is obviously not much point in advertising in a gardening magazine if you are selling road haulage services, or sending a mailshot to all the electrical contractors in your area if you are selling handmade wooden toys. However, it may be less clear which of the following will be the most effective means of promoting your business:

- advertising in newspapers, journals or directories;
- mailshots;
- leaflets and brochures;
- trade shows, exhibitions and fairs.

It is almost impossible to evaluate which option is likely to generate maximum additional business, and you will probably find that a mix of some or all of these is most productive. Of course, some will be more or less appropriate for your particular business. Cost will also be a consideration. For example, a small thatching business with limited financial resources will probably not want to mount an advertising campaign in national newspapers devised by an advertising agency, because the cost of the campaign will be too great weighed against the benefit to the business.

Newspapers, journals and directories

Advertising in newspapers, journals and directories is a reasonably cheap way to reach a fairly large audience. Remember that in most cases you will need to advertise regularly in order to make any impact. If your business is largely seasonal, your advertising can be weighted to the appropriate time of year. A farmer who produces free-range turkeys would choose November and December, for example, to win as much Christmas trade as possible.

Make sure that the content of your advertisement is carefully chosen. Most newspapers and journals will prepare artwork for you, but the content will be your responsibility. Highlight your particular selling points so that they are easy for a reader to pick out. For example, a brief list such as

- competitive prices
- no call-out charge
- 24-hour emergency service
- work guaranteed for 12 months

is much more eye-catching than one long sentence which contains these points. This is largely common sense, and you can look at the 'Classified' section of any newspaper or journal for examples of effective advertisements which stand out. Above all, make sure that your message is clear and concise: remember that you are competing for readers' attention with pages and pages of other advertisements.

Mailshots

Mailshots can be an effective way to reach a very specific potential market, but the average success rate for this type of advertising is just over 1 per cent. Depending on your type of business, there are various ways of sending out mailshots, including:

- delivering leaflets door-to-door;
- sending out material by post by use of a mailing list (which you may buy in or compile yourself);
- arranging for promotional material to be included in a magazine or journal;
- arranging with complementary businesses to have promotional material on show to their customers.

The cost of these options will vary, depending on, for example:

- the design and printing costs of your material;
- whether you need to buy in a mailing list;
- whether you include a 'Reply Paid' card or envelope;
- the distribution costs.

You need to design your promotional material carefully so that it makes an impact on the reader and conveys the image of your business that you want to develop. If it includes a letter as well as a leaflet or brochure, make sure that it is not too long, and where appropriate that it is addressed to the relevant person in the target organization (for example, 'Daniel Taylor, Marketing Director' not 'The Marketing Director').

Leaflets and brochures

Leaflets and brochures describing your product or service can be sent out to existing customers and potential customers in response to sales queries, as well as for more speculative mailshots and to show to suppliers, bankers and other third parties who have an interest in your business. They have the advantage of versatility, since you can use them to pass on information about your business in various different circumstances.

You should research the cost of design and printing with care. It may be tempting to accept the bigger discount available for a print-run of 20,000 copies – but will you realistically use this number before the brochure needs updating?

You must make sure that the content is factually accurate and as up-to-date as possible. The overall presentation is also very important. It should be clear and uncluttered, and give potential customers all the information they need without excessive technical details. The general appearance will also make an impression. You need to assess whether the cost of opting for a very glossy, multi-coloured brochure or leaflet is justified.

Trade shows, exhibitions and fairs

Trade shows and exhibitions can be a good way to meet not only potential new customers, but also suppliers and other contacts. It might help you as well to keep an eye on competitors in your market and their own new developments.

There may not exist a specific show or exhibition which is relevant to your particular business, but you may find that local business associations run general business fairs which are aimed specifically at smaller businesses. Alternatively, you may find that craft fairs are a good way of selling and advertising your product over a wider area and to a wider range of consumers.

A young designer who had recently left college specialized in designing and making hats. Although they were much admired, of a very high quality and competitively priced, she found it difficult to find suitable outlets to sell her work. She was not able to afford the cost of retail premises, and worked from home. A friend suggested she should try exhibiting at a craft fair, where her costs would be more reasonable. Although her sales were not spectacular, they were adequate, and gave her the opportunity to display her work to a much larger audience than would otherwise have been the case. She now travels to a large number of fairs, which have become an excellent source of business for her, and has promotional leaflets and business cards available for distribution to ensure her name becomes known to as many potential customers as possible.

Of course, you will have to weigh up the cost of a stand at a show or exhibition against the potential benefits. Remember that as well as the financial cost, you will also have to devote your time to be available on the stand. If you are working entirely on your own, you will have to assess whether you can afford that time.

As well as the time spent at the show itself, you will also need to spend time afterwards following up – without fail – all the enquiries and sales leads you received at the show. Remember that to recoup at least some of the costs of the show, you will need to make sure you generate additional sales in the longer term.

Most businesses find that a combination of different types of advertising is the most effective way to reach potential new customers. Don't forget, however, that personal recommendations from existing customers can be a very productive source of new business, and that you can work to promote your business even in your most basic day-to-day activities and dealings with suppliers, bankers and business contacts.

Protecting your product

The majority of businesses sell a product or service which is available in similar forms from a number of other sources. These might range from selling stationery or carpets or tooling machinery to offering plumbing or taxi or public relations services. On the other hand, you may have developed a new product or 'invention' which you believe has significant selling potential, and you want to ensure that no one else is able to steal or copy your idea or technology. It is obviously extremely difficult to monitor the developments and products of your immediate competitors constantly, but you can take steps to give your invention some legal protection.

If your design is either entirely new or you want to identify it as your own, you can protect it by applying for a patent, or by registering a design or trade mark.

To qualify as a patentable invention, certain criteria must be met. Broadly, these are:

- it must be new, and not previously known or made public;
- it must be inventive, and not just an improvement or refinement to something which already exists;
- it must have some practical application: it cannot be simply an idea or theory;

• it must not fall within certain excluded categories.

Patents are granted by the Patent Office, which is a government body. Taking out a patent will give you legal protection against the commercial use by others of your invention without your permission. It is essential if you are intending to apply for a patent that you do not divulge your invention to *any* third parties other than a patent agent or in your application to the Patent Office. If you do so, you may invalidate your application.

Taking out a patent is a process involving a number of stages and the payment of fees during the application and investigation period. The process can be a fairly prolonged and complicated one: you can obtain full details from the Patent Office (telephone 01633 814000). You will probably find that a patent agent can offer considerable help and advice, but do ensure that the agent you select is a member of the Chartered Institute of Patent Agents. You can obtain a list of names from the Institute (telephone 0171 405 9450).

If you want to register an original and unusual design, rather than an invention, you should apply to the Designs Registry of the Patent Office. By registering your design, you will gain a better degree of protection than that afforded to you automatically by design right, which operates in a similar way to copyright. Again, a fee will be charged for registration.

To create a distinctive identity for your product, you might choose to use a trade mark which will distinguish your product from others on the market. You need to apply to have your trade mark registered at the Trade Marks Registry; the mark itself can be a word, name or symbol. You will need to consider very carefully the design of your trade mark, to ensure that it conveys the image of your product that you want your customers to retain in their minds. Once again, the process of registration takes some time, and a fee will be charged depending on the number of different classes of products on which you want to use your mark.

8 **If things go wrong . . .**

It is a sad fact that a number of businesses do fail every year, and that new and small businesses are particularly vulnerable whether economic conditions are good or poor. Failure may be the result of bad luck or of management mistakes, but whatever the reasons, no business owner should ever underestimate the distress it causes. On a more positive note, business failure rarely happens overnight, and if you are aware of the danger signs and prepared to acknowledge them you will often have enough time to consider your options and plan how best to proceed.

All new business owners obviously want to make a success of their venture, and invest a great deal of time and energy trying to build up a profitable and stable business: failure will be far from your thoughts. However, if it does begin to emerge that your business is running into difficulties, do not *above all* try to solve your problems by pretending they do not exist. If you refuse to accept them, you will probably be making a positive contribution to your business's failure. If, on the other hand, you are prepared to acknowledge them, talk to the affected parties and seek help quickly enough, you may find you can formulate a plan for survival.

Further reading

The Advisory, Conciliation and Arbitration Service, *Employing People – a handbook for small firms* – 18 advisory bookets and three advisory handbooks available as a collection for around £5 from ACAS.

The Employment Department – series of booklets on employment legislation available from Employment Offices, Unemployment Benefit Offices, and regional offices of the Employment Service.

Institute of Personnel Management – series of *Statements, Codes of Practice* and *Guides* covering a range of employment issues from equal opportunities to redundancy.

John Argenti, *Corporate Collapse – the causes and symptoms*, McGraw-Hill Book Company (UK) Limited, 1976.

Colin and Paul Barrow, *The Business Plan Workbook*, Kogan Page, 1988.

Helen Beare, *How to Avoid Business Failure*, Sheldon Press, 1993.

Richard Denny, *Selling to Win*, Kogan Page, 1988.

Jan Matthews and Nigel Eastaway, *Simplified Assessing*, Tolley Publishing Company Limited, 1994. An in-depth technical guide to the new self-assessment taxation provisions.

Martin Mendelsohn, *The Guide to Franchising*, 5th edition, Cassell, 1993.

David Patten, *Successful Marketing for the Small Business, The Daily Telegraph Guide*, Kogan Page, 1989.

Geoffrey Randall, *Effective Marketing*, Routledge, 1994.

Index

Index